世界に教えたい日本のごはん

WASHOKU

An Illustrated Guide to Japanese Food

淡交社

いただきます！

　ユネスコが無形文化遺産に登録した「和食」。その４つの特徴には「多様で新鮮な食材とその持ち味の尊重」、「健康的な食生活を支える栄養バランス」、「自然の美しさや季節の移ろいの表現」、そして「正月などの年中行事との密接な関わり」があります。

　米と豊かな発酵技術に恵まれた東アジアの食文化圏のなか、1000年以上の肉食禁止や、海外の食文化との出会いによって、現在の和食は形づくられました。和漢の境、和洋の境をまぎらわせて多様化してきた日本文化の、もっともおいしい面白さが「和食」には結晶しています。この本ではそれを、和洋の言葉と絵で世界に伝えます。

ITADAKIMASU!

"*Washoku*" or Japanese cuisine is registered as an "intangible cultural heritage" by UNESCO. It is recognized for the following four notable characteristics; a deep respect for various fresh ingredients and their natural flavors, a nutritional balance that supports a healthy diet, an emphasis on the beauty of nature and the seasons, and a deep connection to traditional annual events such as New Year's Day. Rice and sophisticated fermentation techniques are prevalent throughout East Asia, but washoku as we know it today has been shaped by over a millennia of meat prohibition, followed by a sudden introduction to foreign cuisines. It is a crystallization of the deliciously interesting ways in which Japanese culture has diversified itself through the seamless internalization of external influences, particularly from China and the West. Written in Japanese and English and accompanied with hearty illustrations throughout, this book shares the wonders of Japanese cuisine with the world.

Dishes
料理

Ingredients
食材

Washoku Explained
和食の話

◎参考文献

『日本の食文化史』 石毛直道 (岩波書店)

『東アジアの食事文化』 石毛直道 編 (平凡社)

『東アジアの豆腐づくり』 市野尚子、竹井恵美子 (平凡社)

『日本の香辛料その使い方と歴史』 奥村彪生 (雄山閣)

『吉兆味ばなし 四』 湯木貞一 (暮しの手帖社)

『10品でわかる日本料理』 高橋拓児 (日本経済新聞出版社)

『辻調 感動和食の味わい種明かし帖』 辻芳樹 (小学館)

『発酵はマジックだ』 小泉武夫 (日本経済新聞出版社)

『日本の食はどう変わってきたか』 原田信男 (KADOKAWA)

『日本料理の歴史』 熊倉功夫 (吉川弘文館)

『食卓の文化史』 石毛直道 (岩波書店)

『箸はすごい』 エドワード・ワン 仙名紀 訳 (柏書房)

『和食とは何か』 和食文化ブックレット1 熊倉功夫、江原絢子 (思文閣出版)

『うま味の秘密』 和食文化ブックレット7 伏木亨 (思文閣出版)

『和食と日本酒』 和食文化ブックレット10 増田徳兵衛 (思文閣出版)

『日本の洋食』 青木ゆり子 (ミネルヴァ書房)

『昆布と日本人』 奥井隆 (日本経済新聞出版社)

『日本料理大全』 プロローグ巻 だしとうまみ、調味料
　　特定非営利活動法人日本料理アカデミー 監修 (シュハリ・イニシアティブ株式会社)

『カリスマフード』 畑中三応子 (春秋社)

『だしの神秘』 伏木亨 (朝日新聞出版)

『庖丁』 信田圭造 (ミネルヴァ書房)

『秘められた和食史』 カタジーナ・チフィエルトカ、安原美帆 (新泉社)

『ラーメンの歴史学』 バラク・クシュナー 幾島幸子 訳 (明石書店)

『お好み焼きの物語』 近代食文化研究会 新紀元社

『日本めん食文化の1300年』 奥村彪生 (農文教)

『日本の食文化 4 魚と肉』 藤井弘章 編 (吉川弘文館)

『日本人は寿司のことを何も知らない。』 美しい日本の常識を再発見する会 編 (学研プラス)

『残念和食にもワケがある 写真で見る日本の食卓の今』 岩村暢子 (中央公論新社)

『日本食と出汁 ──ご馳走の文化史』 松本仲子 (雄文閣)

『食べる』 神戸女学院大学文学部 総合文化学科 監修 景山佳代子 編 (世界思想社)

『和食に恋して 和食文化考』 鳥居本幸代 (春秋社)

『「和の食」全史』 永山久夫 (河出書房新社)

JAPANESE COOKING　A SIMPLE ART　Shizuo Tsuji　introduction by M.F.K.Fisher (KODANSHA INTERNATIONAL)

◎協力

株式会社崎陽軒 (P.72)

英文は逐語訳ではなく、自然な英語で翻訳しています
This book is translated to read naturally.

WASHOKU
Dishes

料 理

Katsudon

カツ丼

pork cutlet rice bowl

DONBURI

どんぶり *rice bowl*

Tonkatsu
とんかつ
pork cutlet

Tamago
玉子
egg

Negi
ネギ
green scallion

Gohan
ごはん
rice

Donburi
どんぶり
oversized rice bowl

和食の基本「ご飯とおかず」を重ねていただきます
Rice and Sides in One Bite!

「ご飯とおかず」こそ、和食の究極の二大要素。その２つを一度に頬ばれるどんぶりは、最速で和食の美味しさを楽しめるメニューです。

どんぶりの生まれは、19世紀の江戸。屋台の寿司がファストフードとして人気をよんでいた頃、手軽に食べられる料理として天ぷら屋（P.24）が考案した天丼が最初といわれています。

揚げ物、煮物、刺身、そして洋食。あらゆるおかずが、どんぶりのトッピングになります。人気のカツ丼は、洋食（P.32）のトンカツを、タマネギと一緒に醤油味のダシで煮て、ご飯にのせたもの。香ばしいカツとご飯をダシがとりもちます。

ふっくらした日本のジャポニカ米（P.98）は、あらゆるおかずと一体になり、その包容力が、どんぶりのおいしさの要。和食のおかずは、口の中でごはんと一緒になった時にこそ、おいしいように調理されています。ご飯とおかずを口の中で合わせて味を完成させる「口中調味」は和食に特徴的な味わい方で、その効果を最速で実感させてくれるメニューもまた、どんぶりなのです。

The two foundational pillars of Japanese cuisine are rice and savory side dishes, which are made to taste delicious when combined in the mouth. The *donburi* or rice bowl unites these two elements, and is one of the most efficient ways to enjoy the flavors of Japanese cuisine. The rice bowl was born in the city of *Edo*—now known as Tokyo—in the 19th century. At the time, *sushi* served at food-stands was gaining popularity as a fast-food.

The very first donburi is said to have entered the scene when the owner of a *tempura* restaurant (*P.24*) came up with the *tendon*, or tempura rice bowl, as a quick alternative to the traditional format.

The *katsudon* is a bowl of rice topped with pork *katsu* (*P.33*) and onions simmered with soy sauce and *dashi* stock, which balances the savory katsu with rice. Japonica rice (*P.98*) has a slightly viscous quality that carries the flavors of the ingredients well, and it is the shining star of this dish.

Tonkatsu
とんかつ *pork cutlet*

トンカツ（カツ）は、タマネギと一緒に醤油味のダシで煮て味をつける。エビカツやビーフカツをのせたり、ダシの代わりにソースや味噌味のタレを染み込ませたどんぶりもある

The tonkatsu or katsu, which is deep-fried breaded pork cutlet, is simmered with onions and dashi broth seasoned with soy sauce. Some donburis feature shrimp or beef katsu instead of pork, and some are drizzled with Japanese Worcestershire sauce or *miso*-based sauce.

Tamago
玉子 *egg*

煮汁に玉子を溶き入れ、半熟にして、ふんわりとさせた状態でカツを覆う。これは「玉子とじ」と呼ばれる料理法で、うどん（P.46）、煮物（P.78）などにも使われる

Beaten eggs are added to the broth at the end to bind the ingredients together in a soft, fluffy cloud. This technique is known as "tamago-toji" and is applied in other dishes such as *udon* (*P.46*) or *nimono* (*P.78*).

Negi
ネギ *scallion*

緑（または白）のネギは、色彩と香りを添える薬味で、味噌汁や麺類など、多くの和食で活躍する。薬味ネギのほか、鍋の具材などに使う太い白ネギもある

Green (or white, see *P.66*) scallion is used as a condiment for many Japanese dishes, such as miso soup and noodles to add color and fragrance.

Gohan
ご飯 *rice*

ご飯は粘りがあって、冷めてもおいしいジャポニカ米(P.98)なので、どんぶりはテイクアウトの食事としても重宝される

Sticky Japonica rice (*P.98*) is just as delicious when it cools, which makes donburi a popular take-out item.

Donburi
どんぶり *oversized rice bowl*

「どんぶり」はこの器の意味でもある。どこの家庭にでもあり、麺類などにも使われる

The term "donburi" also refers to the type of vessel itself. It is found in every household and used for a variety of dishes including noodles.

Rice Bowl Variations
どんぶりのいろいろ

Tendon
天丼
tempura bowl

Oyakodon
親子丼
chiken and egg bowl

　世界でもっとも有名などんぶりは牛丼。牛肉を醤油、砂糖、みりんで甘辛く炊いて煮汁と一緒にご飯にかける牛丼は、チェーン店の海外進出のおかげで、ユニバーサルなメニューになりました。日本で人気のどんぶりには、鶏肉を"子供"の玉子でとじた親子丼、玉子だけの玉子丼、海老や穴子、野菜などの天ぷらをのせた天丼などがあります。トッピングはダシで煮てご飯にのせるクラシックなスタイルのほか、刺身をのせる海鮮丼はわさび醤油をかけて、ハンバーグ

とサラダをのせたロコモコ丼はグレービーソースをかけます。ロコモコ丼は、ハワイの日系人が考案して日本に逆輸入されました。このほか、メキシコのタコライスやベジタリアンのブッダボウルなど、海外からもどんぶりのニューウェーブが到来し、各地の名物をのせた日本の多彩なご当地どんぶりと共存しています。

　どんなトッピングも自由自在。ご飯の上に乗れば、なんでも和食になれる。それが、どんぶりマジックです。

Kaisendon
海鮮丼
sashimi bowl

Locomocodon
ロコモコ丼
locomoco

The most celebrated donburi is no doubt the *gyudon*, or beef bowl. The rice is topped with piping hot beef simmered in a sweet and savory soy sauce-based broth, juices and all. Thanks to many franchise businesses, today the beef bowl is enjoyed widely across the globe. Other popular donburis include *oyakodon* or chicken and egg bowl, the egg-only *tamagodon*, and tendon—a medley of tempura such as shrimp and conger eel over rice. The toppings are prepared in a variety of ways; it can be simmered in broth, or drizzled with *wasabi*-soy sauce in the case of *kaisendon*. The locomocodon is a rice bowl topped with Hamburg steak, salad, and gravy. Initially invented by Japanese immigrants in Hawaii, it is a popular dish in Japan today. There are also new wave rice bowls influenced by foreign cuisines, such as the Mexican influenced "taco-rice bowl" and the vegetarian "Buddha bowl," which have joined the countless local varieties native to Japan. Any topping is fair game, and even foreign foods become Japanese cuisine when served over rice. This is the magic of the rice bowl!

SUSHI

寿司 *sushi*

Nigirizushi

握り寿司 *nigiri sushi*

Murasaki

むらさき *high quality soy sauce*

Ikura
いくら
salmon roe

Akagai
赤貝
ark shell clam

Ika
イカ *squid*

Uni
ウニ *sea urchin*

Menegi
ネギ *menegi scallion*

Maguro
鮪 *tuna*

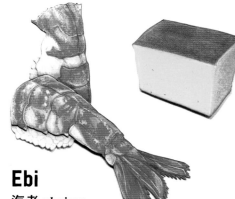

Tamagoyaki
玉子焼き
sweet omelet

Ebi
海老 *shrimp*

Gari
ガリ *pickled ginger*

Toro
トロ *fatty tuna*

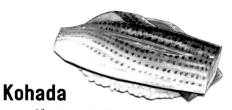

Kohada
コハダ *gizzard shad*

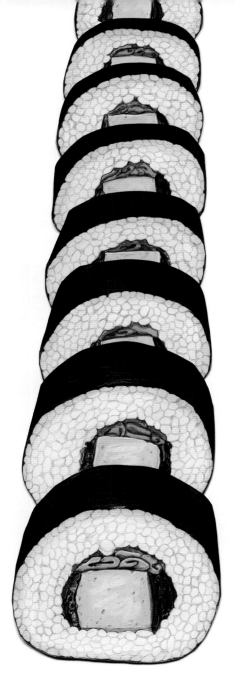

Makizushi
巻き寿司 *rolled sushi*

Nori
海苔 *nori seaweed*

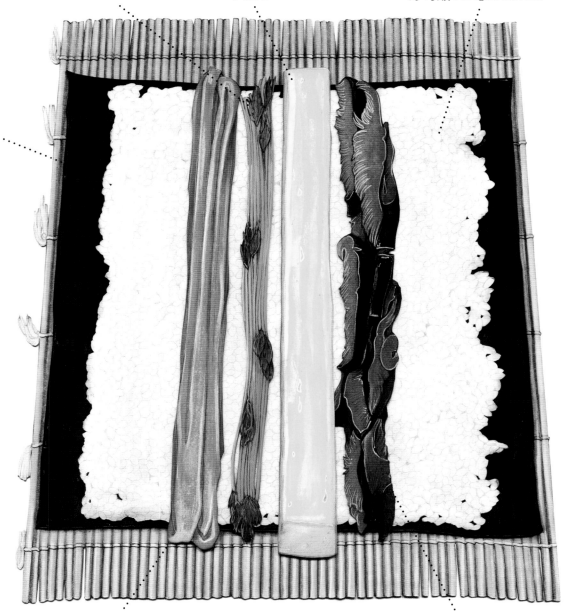

Mitsuba
ミツバ *Japanese honewort*

Tamagoyaki
玉子焼き *sweet omelet*

Sushimeshi
寿司飯 *vinegared rice*

Kanpyo
干瓢 *dried gourd*

Hoshi Shiitake
干しシイタケ
dried shiitake mushroom

1000年かけて、スローフードがファストフードに
Over a Millennia, a Slow Food Becomes Fast Food

　世界で人気の寿司。なぜ酸っぱいご飯に魚がのっているのか、ご存じでしょうか？　寿司のルーツは魚をご飯で発酵させた「なれずし」。"なれ"とは発酵のことで、広く東南アジアで親しまれてきた保存食です。日本では、平安時代（794〜1185）からつくられていて、琵琶湖（滋賀県）のふなずしは、当時の姿を今に伝えています。魚だけを食べるものだったなれずしが、発酵したご飯もあわせて食べるようになり、後に発酵を省略してご飯を酢で酸っぱくしました。それが現在の寿司飯です。握り寿司は18世紀の江戸で、屋台の人気スナックになりました。発酵食というスローフードから、ファストフードへの進化です。

　気軽な携帯食から近年、行事食に進化したのが巻き寿司です。節分の日に縁起のいい方角に向かって巻き寿司を丸かぶりして幸運を祈る「恵方巻（えほうまき）」は、1998年にコンビニエンスストアが全国展開して以来、国民的な行事となっています。

Sushi today is a popular dish worldwide, but not many people know how the fish came to sit atop vinegared rice. The origin of sushi was *narezushi*, a traditional food where fish is fermented in rice. "Nare" means fermentation, but this traditional method of fermenting fish with rice is found throughout Asian cultures. Japan's narezushi goes back to the *Heian* period (794-1185), and still remains today as *funazushi*, a specialty food made near Lake Biwa (Shiga Prefecture). Initially only the fish was eaten, but people became accustomed to also eating the fermented rice, and eventually started vinegaring rice as a quick alternative to the fermentation process. Thus, sushi rice was born. After this key evolution changed the fermented slow food into fast food, *nigiri* sushi became a popular snack in 18th century Edo (now Tokyo).

Makizushi, or rolled sushi, was another innovation that happened as the sushi became a popular food for special occasions. *Ehomaki* is an annual custom of eating makizushi for good luck; it is eaten whole as one faces the lucky direction of the year on *Setsubun*, a day that marks the beginning of spring. It was popularized and embraced as a tradition across the country after convenience stores rolled out nationwide in 1998.

Nori

海苔 *nori seaweed sheet*

海苔は品質によって細かく等級が
定められていて、寿司には高級な海
苔を用いる。巻く前に片面をあぶっ
て、香ばしさを引き立てる

Nori is graded very precisely by
quality. Sushi requires higher grade
nori, which is toasted before use on
one side to bring out the fragrance.

Tamagoyaki

玉子焼き *sweet omelet*

寿司屋の玉子焼きにはダシと砂糖
で甘く焼いたもの、または魚やエビ
のすり身、大和芋を加えてカステラ
のように厚く焼いた厚焼きなどがあ
る。大阪や、その他の地域では玉子
焼きの代わりに、あるいは一緒に高
野豆腐を巻くこともある

At sushi restaurants, the omelet is
cooked sweet with dashi and sugar.
Some restaurants add fish or shrimp
paste, or add grated yamato potato
to make a thick, almost cake-like
omelet. Some restaurants in Osaka
and other areas use dehydrated
koyadofu as a substitute or together
with the egg.

Mitsuba

ミツバ *Japanese honewort*

茹でたミツバは色と歯ごたえのアク
セント。キュウリを使うことも

Also called Japanese parsley, mitsuba is cooked and added for color
and texture. Some restaurants use
cucumber instead.

Sushimeshi

寿司飯 *vinegared rice*

寿司用語で「シャリ」と呼ばれる。
米を昆布と一緒に炊いて、酢と砂
糖、塩で味をつける。これにより、
米粒が調味料でコーティングされて
風味と保存性が高められる

Also called "shari," sushi rice is
cooked with *kombu* kelp and seasoned with vinegar, sugar, and salt.
Coating the rice with this seasoning
deepens the flavors and allows the
rice to keep longer.

Hoshi Shiitake

干しシイタケ
dried shiitake mushroom

干したシイタケを戻した汁をダシと
して使いながら、醤油とみりん、砂
糖で甘く煮る

The *shiitake* mushrooms are rehydrated before they are simmered in
the same water which is rich in
mushroom umami, along with soy
sauce, mirin, and sugar.

Kanpyo

干瓢
dried gourd

ウリ科の野菜の果肉を乾燥させたも
の。戻して醤油とみりん *(P.108)* 、砂
糖で煮る

Dried gourd meat, rehydrated and
simmered with soy sauce, mirin,
and sugar.

Chirashizushi

ちらし寿司 *scattered sushi*

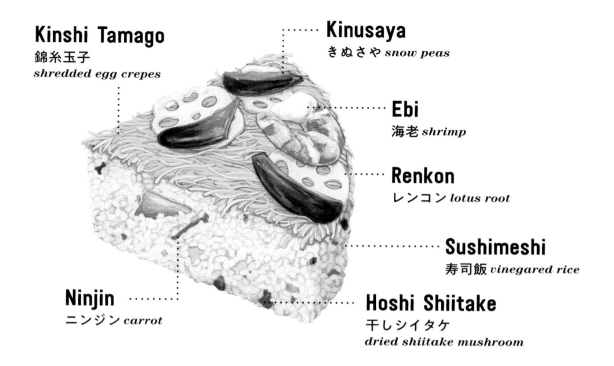

Kinshi Tamago
錦糸玉子
shredded egg crepes

Kinusaya
きぬさや *snow peas*

Ebi
海老 *shrimp*

Renkon
レンコン *lotus root*

Sushimeshi
寿司飯 *vinegared rice*

Hoshi Shiitake
干しシイタケ
dried shiitake mushroom

Ninjin
ニンジン *carrot*

握らない、巻かない、温かい。これも寿司
Warm Rice Neither Rolled or Shaped; this is Also Sushi

生の魚を使わない寿司や、温かい寿司もあります。ちらし寿司は、寿司飯に細かく切った野菜や調理した魚介類を混ぜ込み、錦糸玉子などをトッピングしたもの。「まぜ寿し」「ばらずし」とも呼ばれ、その歴史は握り寿司よりも古く、全国各地に、その地の名産品を使ったちらし寿司があります。多くの具材が必要なちらし寿司ですが、家庭では、ご飯に混ぜるだけでできる即席のちらし寿司の素を使って、気軽に作られています。華やかなルックスは、弁当(P.72)やホームパーティーにも活躍します。このちらし寿司を蒸したものが、ほかほかの「蒸し寿司」。京都をはじめ、各地の冬のごちそうです。

Some types of sushi are made with cooked fish, and some are even served warm. *Chirashizushi*, which translates to "scattered sushi," is a type of sushi mixed with minced vegetables and cooked seafood, and topped with shredded egg crepes. Sometimes also called *mazezushi* or *barazushi*, it actually has a longer history than nigiri sushi. It also has wonderful potential for variety, and there are local chirashizushi featuring different specialty ingredients all across the country. Today, instant chirashizushi mixes are sold at supermarkets for casual settings in the home. A bright, colorful dish, it is often the main feature of home parties and *bento* (P.72). *Mushizushi* is a steamed version of chirashizushi, and a specialty of Kyoto among other places.

Otsukuri Moriawase
お造り盛り合わせ
assorted sashimi

SASHIMI

刺身 *sashimi*

Sashimi shoyu 刺身醤油 *sashimi soy sauce* / Wasabi わさび *wasabi*

"料理しない" 最高の料理
The Ultimate "Uncooked" Dish

　和食の最高の料理、それは刺身です。cook ＝火を使った調理といえない生の魚が、なぜ最高の料理なのか？ 日本では、生で食べられる鮮度の高い食材こそが高級とされ、それを美味しく食べるために多くの手間と技術が注がれているのが刺身だからです。刺身の準備は、魚が海から揚がった時から始まります。漁師は「活〆（いけじめ）」と呼ばれる技で魚の神経伝達を遮断して鮮度と食感を保ったまま熟成させます。海に囲まれた日本では数多くの魚介類が手に入ります。料理人は長い年月をかけて魚の鮮度と旬 (*P.94*) を見極める「目利き」の修業をして、その時最もおいしい魚を選び抜き、その魚を、片刃の長い包丁 (*P.100*) を使って一気に引きます。このことから、刺身は「切る」と言わず「引く」と言います。仕上げはケン、シソを添えた盛り付け。立体感を出したこの造形的な美しさから、刺身は「お造り」とも呼ばれます。スーパーマーケットでさえ、お造りはパックの中に繊細に盛り合わせられて売られています。

Sashimi is considered the ultimate washoku dish, but why is such a simple and uncooked dish regarded so highly? In Japan, ingredients that are fresh enough to eat raw are considered more valuable, and sashimi preparation in particular requires substantial labor and technique. Sashimi preparation begins when the fish is first taken out of the sea. The fishermen perform *ikejime*, a technique that shuts off the fish's neurotransmission in order to preserve freshness and texture while the fish matures. Because Japan is surrounded by ocean, a great variety of fish is available. Each fish has its peak, which is referred to as *shun* (*P.94*), and chefs train for years to develop ability to determine whether a fish is fresh and at its peak. The carefully selected fish is cut into smaller pieces in one stoke with a sashimi knife (*P.100*); a long and sharp single-sided knife, which creates a smooth surface. Because the knife is pulled back rather than pushed down, this is described as "pulling sashimi." Finally, the sashimi is delicately arranged and decorated with garnish and perilla leaf. This is why sashimi is also called "*otsukuri*," which means creation or arrangement. Beautifully arranged sashimi are also available in most supermarkets.

Tempura Moriawase
天ぷら盛り合わせ
assorted tempura

Ebi 海老 *shrimp* / Kisu キス *Japanese whiting* / Shiitake シイタケ *shiitake mushroom* / Shishito シシトウ *shishito pepper* / Shiso 大葉 *perilla leaf* / Nasu ナス *eggplant* / Renkon レンコン *lotus root*
Tendashi 天だし *dipping sauce* / Daikon Oroshi 大根おろし *grated daikon radish*

TEMPURA

天ぷら *tempura*

日本でいちばん古い"洋食"?
Japan's Oldest "Western" Dish

　和食を代表する料理・天ぷらは、実は外国からやってきて日本に定着した、元祖・洋食(*P.32*)。揚げ物が日本に初上陸したのは、奈良時代(8世紀)。遣唐使が持ち帰った供物の揚げ菓子でした。鎌倉時代(13世紀頃)には、中国の宋から禅とともに精進料理(*P.106*)の素揚げが伝えられました。現在の天ぷらに近い、小麦粉の衣をつけた揚げ物は、16世紀にキリスト教とともにポルトガルから伝来しました。語源は「料理」を意味するtemperoと言われています。この西洋の揚げ物が和食化したのが天ぷらです。

　天ぷらは、揚げ物でありながら、いかに軽く、そして素材の鮮度と風味を生かすかが、技の見せどころ。天ぷら専門店では、修業を積んだ職人が、ごく薄い衣をつけ、敷き紙に油が付かないほどからりと天ぷらを揚げ、お客は揚げたてをいただきます。大根おろし(*P.95*)と天だし、または塩をつけます。

Tempura, a dish representative of Japanese cuisine, is actually one of the earliest forms of *yoshoku* (*P.32*). Deep fried foods first introduced in the 8th century during the *Nara* period (8th c.), when Japanese envoys brought fried desserts made for altar offerings. Around the 13th century during the *Kamakura* period, *suage* (a batterless deep fried dish), which is part of *shojin ryori* (*P.106*), was brought over from *Song* dynasty China along with *Zen* Buddhism. Tempura evolved from battered deep fried foods that came from Portugal along with Christianity, during the 16th century. The term tempura is said to have come from the Portuguese word "*tempero*," which means to season or to cook.

Though tempura is a fried food, it is important to cook it so that the batter is airy, and the ingredients taste fresh. At tempura specialty restaurants, seasoned chefs coat the ingredients very lightly and fry them so crisp that hardly any oil transfers to the sheet of paper upon which they are served. Enjoy with grated *daikon* radish (*P.95*) and dipping sauce, or simply with salt.

Sansho 山椒 *Japanese pepper* / Kimosui 肝吸い *eel organ soup* / Unaju うな重 *unagi over rice* / Tsukemono 漬物 *pickles*

Unaju
うな重
eel over rice in "jubako" lacquer box

UNAGI

鰻 *eel*

100年もののタレ香る、日本最古のスタミナ食
An Ancient Stamina-Boosting Food and its 100-Year-Old Sauce

鰻は日本最古の国民的スタミナ食。奈良時代（8世紀）の昔にも、歌集『万葉集』に「夏痩せには、鰻を取って食べよ」という意味の歌が収められています。夏の初めの土用の丑の日（7月下旬）には精をつけて夏を乗り切るために鰻を食べる習慣があり、スーパーやコンビニでも鰻の蒲焼やどんぶりが売り出されます。

蛇のように長くヌルヌルした鰻の腹を裂いて串を打ち、炭火で焼くのは職人の技。皮はこんがり、身がふんわりとした蒲焼を焼くための修業は、「串打ち3年、裂き8年、焼き一生」と言われます。蒲焼のたまらない香ばしさは、みりん（P.108）と醤油がベースのタレに秘密があります。専門店では、鰻をこのタレの壺の中に浸けながら焼きます。そうすることでタレに脂や旨みが加わり、さらにそれを長年注ぎ足して使い続けることで、お店秘伝の味になります。老舗の中には、100年以上注ぎ足し続けたタレを誇る店もあります。

Eel, or *unagi*, has been regarded as a power food since ancient times and is enjoyed all over the country today. A poem in the *Manyoshu*, a collection of poetry compiled during the Nara period tells us to catch and eat an eel when the summer heat causes wasting. Today, there is a tradition of eating eel on a special day in mid-summer (usually late July) in order to nourish the body and get through the hot summer. Eel is sold widely in supermarkets and even convenience stores during this time.

The long, snake-like slippery eel is split down the stomach, skewered, and delicately grilled over charcoal fire. It is said that mastering the art of grilling an eel to fluffy perfection takes one "three years to skewer, 8 years to split, and a lifetime to grill." The secret of the irresistible savory aroma lies in the soy sauce and *mirin* (*P.108*) -based sauce. At traditional eel restaurants, the eel is dipped into a large clay pot of sauce as it is grilled. This adds the goodness and umami of the eel to the sauce, which is repeatedly replenished and used over many years to create the restaurant's own "secret sauce." Some long-standing eel restaurants take pride in dipping sauces that have been matured for over a hundred years.

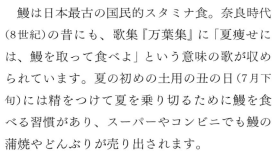

Yakizakana Teishoku

焼き魚定食 *grilled fish set meal*

TEISHOKU

定食 *set meal*

意外と歴史は新しい、和食の完全バランス・一汁三菜
The Perfect Balance of a Japanese Set Meal

　ユネスコ無形文化遺産に登録された和食。高く評価されたポイントの一つが「健康的な食生活」です。和食の献立の基本は、ご飯と味噌汁、肉や魚の主菜と、野菜、漬物（P.88）などの副菜からなる「一汁三菜」です。これは、江戸時代（1603〜1868）の武家のもてなし料理「本膳料理」が、ご飯と汁に三菜を添えていたことに由来します。しかし当時は、武士の家庭でさえ、おかずが3品並ぶことは稀で、食事は白米に偏っていました。明治時代（1868〜1912）以降、日本は西洋的な肉食、野菜、料理法を取り入れることで、栄養状態を改善。栄養バランスのいい「一汁三菜」は、1950年代以降になって一般家庭に定着しました。食堂（P.110）のメニュー、定食も、この「一汁三菜」で構成されています。定食を食べる時には、ご飯茶碗を片手に持って、おかずとご飯と味噌汁を、順番に口に運んでください。これは「三角食べ」と言われる食べ方で、和食のマナーであり、ご飯を中心とした和食をバランスよく味わうコツでもあります。

　Japanese food or "wahsoku" is registered as an intangible cultural heritage by UNESCO, particularly because of its many health benefits. "*Ichiju sansai*," which means one soup and three dishes, is a word that describes the basic structure of a Japanese meal; rice, soup, a fish or meat main dish, pickles (*P.88*) and vegetable sides. This term refers back to *honzen-ryori*, which was served to entertain the samurai class during the Edo period, but in reality most meals were heavy on the rice, and it was rare even for the samurai to enjoy three sides. However, once the country entered the *Meiji* period (1868-1912), the nation's nutritional status was greatly improved upon incorporating Western vegetables and customs of eating meat. The ichiju sansai format was recognized and embraced in the home as a well-balanced meal after the 1950s, and *teishoku* set meals served in *shokudo* (*P.110*) are faithful to this format. One is to hold the bowl of rice in one hand, and alternate between eating the rice, miso soup, and main and side dishes with the other hand. This "triangular eating" is not only an important etiquette in Japanese cuisine, but also a great trick for balancing Japanese flavors.

Teishoku Elements
定食の組み合わせ

Tsukemono
漬物 *pickles* (P.88)

Kobachi : Ohitashi
小鉢：おひたし
side dish : vegetables seasoned with dashi and soy sauce (P.76)

Shusai
主菜 *main dish*

Gohan
ごはん *rice* (P.98)

Misoshiru
味噌汁 *miso soup with tofu and scallion* (P.108)

Aji-furai
アジフライ
deep fried horse mackerel

Buta-no-shougayaki
豚の生姜焼き
ginger pork

Tori-no-karaage
鶏の唐揚げ
fried chicken

Tonkatsu
とんかつ
pork cutlet

YOSHOKU

洋食 *Japanese Western cuisine*

Omuraisu

オムライス

omelet rice

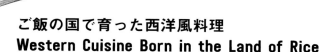

ご飯の国で育った西洋風料理
Western Cuisine Born in the Land of Rice

「洋食」は、西洋料理と思われがちですが、ど
この国にもない日本の料理。そして実は、「洋
食」がなければ「和食」という言葉もありませ
んでした。明治時代（1868〜1912）、日本政府
は富国強兵策として、栄養豊富な西洋の食を推
奨しました。これ以降、肉、フライ、ソースや
香辛料など、新たに日本の食に入ってきた西洋
風の味は洋食と呼ばれ、同時にそれまでにあっ
た日本の料理が「和食」と呼ばれるようになっ
たのです。ご飯の国・日本は、西洋料理からイ
ンスピレーションを得て、数々の独創的な「ラ
イスもの」メニューを生み出しました。チキン
ライスやピラフなどを薄焼きの卵料理のオムレ
ットに包んだオムライス、ハッシュドビーフを
ご飯にかけたハヤシライス、そしてライスグラ
タンのドリア。魚や肉にパン粉の衣をつけて少
量の油で揚げ焼きするフランス料理のコートレ
ットを応用して、天ぷら（P.24）のようにたっぷ
りの油で揚げたカツは、お箸で食べられるよう
に切って出されます。こうした代表的な洋食は、
名前は洋でも、味もプレゼンテーションも「和
食」そのもの。洋食に欠かせないウスターソー
スは、イギリスのウースターシャソースをモデ
ルにしたものですが、食卓にボトルを置いて、
フライやカレーライスにお好みでかけて食べる
という使い方には、日本の「かけ醤油」（P.108）
の習慣が反映されています。

As part of its policy to increase national pros-
perity and military power, the Meiji government
(1868-1912) recommended Western cuisine as a
nutritionally superior diet. This is when the terms
"yoshoku" and "washoku" were born to differenti-
ate the new Western-inspired dishes featuring meat,
fried foods, condiments such as Worcestershire
sauce, spices, and so forth, from traditional Japanese cuisine. Many classic yoshoku dishes are
rice-centered, like *omuraisu*, which is chicken rice or
pilaf covered with a thin omelet, and *hayashiraisu*,
which is simmered thin-cut beef in demi-glace-based
stew over rice. Katsu, similar to tempura (*P.24*), is
breaded and deep-fried fish or meat. Originally
inspired by the French *côtelette*, it is also a classic
yoshoku item. However, despite the Western elements, both the flavors and presentation of such
yoshoku dishes are distinctly Japanese. Even Japanese Worcestershire sauce—a Japanese take on the
British Worcestershire sauce often referred to simply as "sauce"—has a similar status to the ultimate
Japanese condiment, soy sauce. It is an important
companion to deep fried dishes, curries, and other
yoshoku dishes, and a bottle is often kept out on the
table the same way one keeps a bottle of soy sauce
(*P.108*) handy for a washoku meal.

Yoshoku Classics
定番洋食のいろいろ

Korokke
コロッケ
croquette

Katsu Kareraisu
カツカレーライス
curry rice topped with pork cutlet

　洋食は、様々な国から来て、日本化しました。インドを植民地にしていたイギリス海軍から伝わったカレーは、ご飯にかける日本式カレーライスになりました。付け合わせの赤い福神漬け（p.88）は、インドの漬物、チャツネを真似たものと言われます。

　コロッケはフランス国王ルイ14世の料理人が考案したベシャメルソースのクロケットが起源だといわれていますが、日本ではそれに近いクリームコロッケよりも、つぶしたジャガイモを丸めて油で揚げるコロッケのほうが一般的です。ハンバーグはドイツ北部の港町ハンブルグの肉料理が、移民によってアメリカに伝わり、日本では大正時代（1912-1926）に広まりました。現代では家庭料理として定着し、大根おろしやテリヤキ味で、さらに日本化が進んでいます。イタリアのスパゲティは、明太子や納豆など日本の食材と融合して、和風の麺料理になっています。スパゲティをケチャップで具材と炒めたナポリタンは、焼きそば（P.58）風の料理ですが、その焼きそばは、中国由来の料理です。

　洋食の専門店には、創業100年を超える老舗もあり、和洋の境を超えた日本の伝統食として受け継がれています。

Hanbagu
ハンバーグ
Hamburg steak

Naporitan Supagetti
ナポリタンスパゲッティ
Napolitan spaghetti

Japanese Western cuisine encompasses a wide variety of influences. The Japanese curry-rice was introduced by the British Royal Navy, and its condiment, *fukujinzuke* (*P.88*) is inspired by chutney, a type of condiment used in Indian cuisines. The Japanese *croquette* or *korokke* was inspired by the French béchamel-sauce filled croquette, which was originally devised by one of King Louis XIV's chefs. In Japan, the korokke is most commonly made by frying breaded mashed potatoes mixed with meat or vegetables. The *hambagu*, also known as the Japanese Hamburg steak, was inspired by a meat dish from the port town of Hamburg in northern Germany, which was introduced to the U.S. by immigrants and brought to Japan during the *Taisho* period (1912-1926). It has since evolved to partner with Japanese-style flavors such as grated daikon radish or *teriyaki* sauce. The Italian spaghetti has also been integrated as a vehicle for Japanese flavors such as *mentaiko* (spicy cod roe) and *natto* (fermented soy bean) as well as Western flavors. The Naporitan spaghetti is a classic yoshoku pasta dish; the noodles are cooked in a ketchup-based sauce and topped with parmesan cheese, similar to the way *yakisoba* (*P.58*) is prepared. Some long-established yoshoku restaurants have been in business for over 100 years.

CHUKA

中華料理 *Japanese Chinese cuisine*

Gyoza
餃子
*pan fried
dumpling*

中国生まれで日本育ち。GYOZA は "中華" の国際スター
Gyoza, the International Star of Japanese Chinese Cuisine

　唐揚げ、麻婆豆腐、酢豚など、日本の家庭料理には中国料理をルーツとするメニューが多く見られます。中国料理の看板を掲げる大衆店のお品書きは、ご飯に中国風の料理をのせた「中華丼」など、多くが日本生まれの「中華料理」です。薄い皮の焼き餃子も、和食化した中国料理です。中国の餃子は、厚い皮であんを包んで茹でて食べる、麺料理のようなスタイル。それを日本では、ご飯のおかずになるように皮のボリュームを薄く抑えて香ばしく焼いたのです。ラーメン（P.50）や餃子は、今では日本名で海外進出を果たし、世界中の旅行者が、"本場の味"を楽しみに来日します。こうした外来の食べ物の巧みなアレンジは日本に独特なイノベーションだと言われますが、タイのカオマンガイ、シンガポールの海南チキンライス、インドネシアのミーゴレンなど、アジア諸国には中国料理を進化させた国民的な料理が数多くあります。

　Japanese home cooking features many Chinese-influenced dishes known as "*chuka*," such as *karaage* fried chicken, *mabo tofu*, and *subuta* sweet and sour pork. *Chukadon*, a rice bowl topped with Chinese-style stir-fry, and other chuka dishes are served in casual Chinese restaurants all over Japan. *Gyoza*, the Japanese version of Chinese dumplings, are wrapped in a thin dough and pan-fried. While Chinese dumplings are wrapped in a thicker dough, boiled, and eaten more as a main dish, the Japanese version is modified to accompany rice. Today, *ramen* (*P.50*) and gyoza are popular around the world and many tourists come to Japan to enjoy the "authentic" flavors. Both yoshoku and chuka are considered clever culinary inventions specific to Japan, but many Asian countries have national dishes that evolved from Chinese food, such as Thailand's *khao man gai*, Singapore's Hainanese chicken rice, and Indonesia's *mi goreng*.

KAISEKI RYORI

会席料理 *kaiseki course meal*

茶の湯の懐石と会席料理

　会席料理は、17世紀に成立した酒宴の饗応（宴会）料理・本膳料理に源流がみられます。これに、季節感を大切に旬の素材を活かし楽しむ茶席の料理「懐石」のエッセンスが加えられました。温かいものは温かく、冷たいものは冷たいままで一品ずつ調理法をかえて丁寧に作って出される、茶の湯のこころがこもった料理・懐石が取り込まれているのです。そのため、会席料理を「懐石料理」としている店も多くみられます。料亭 *(P.110)*「吉兆」の湯木貞一(1901-1997)が、「お茶の料理は、日本料理の片隅にありながら、日本料理を支配するほどの力を持っている」と語っていたように、茶の湯の懐石は日本料理に大きな影響を与えたのです。華やかな器 *(P.104)* で登場する会席料理のハイライトは、旬の食材を美しく盛り合わせた八寸、向付、椀もの。驚く人もいるかもしれませんが、実はこのお椀の吸いものが、コースの主役です。

Shokuji 食事 *rice & pickles* | Agemono 揚げ物 *deep fried dish* | Yakimono 焼き物 *grilled dish* | Wanmono 椀もの *clear soup* | Hassun 八寸 *small seasonal dish* | Nimono 煮物 *simmered dish* | Mukouzuke 向付 *sashimi*

The Two Kaiseki: Tea Ceremony Kaiseki and Kaiseki Ryori

Kaiseki ryori, written as "会席料理," is a classic meal format within Japanese cuisine. It evolved from a type of banquet meal from the 17th century called honzen-ryori, but also includes elements of *cha-kaiseki* or tea ceremony *kaiseki* (written as "懐石"), which emphasizes the four seasons and features peak ingredients. In the spirit of tea ceremony, cha-kaiseki dishes are served one by one at their appropriate temperature with precision and care. For this reason, many traditional restaurants use the characters for *cha*-kaiseki to describe their cuisine. As Yuki Teiichi (1901-1997), founder of the *ryotei* (*P.110*) "Kitcho" is known to have said, "although tea ceremony kaiseki sits in a niche within Japanese cuisine, it also has the power to rule it." Indeed, tea ceremony kaiseki has had a tremendous impact on Japanese cuisine. The highlight of kaiseki ryori which is served in elaborate vessels (*P.104*), are the *hassun*, a delicate arrangement of seasonal ingredients, *mukouzuke* or sashimi, and *wanmono*, a clear soup, which perhaps to the surprise of many, is considered the main feature of the meal.

暖簾から読める、お店のメッセージ
Reading the Messages in a Restaurant's Fabric Divider

料理店の入り口のカーテン、暖簾。掛けられていれば店が営業中ということを表します。その素材やデザインはさりげなく店の格やセンスを伝え、夏と冬とで掛け替えることで季節感を表現します。暖簾は内と外とを分けるサインで、店内にある「内暖簾」は、客席と厨房の間の仕切りを意味します。また、内暖簾が扉の内に掛かっている場合は「一見さんはお断り」というメッセージです。暖簾は店の象徴で、店を発展させることを「暖簾を大きくする」と言います。

硬派なムード漂う「割烹」の暖簾。割烹はご主人とカウンター越しに対面して食事する、居酒屋 (P.110) よりもプライベートな食事処。
A classic noren hung outside a kappo restaurant. At kappo restaurants, guests sit at the counter in front of the chef for a more private and intimate dining experience than izakaya (P.110).

A *noren* is a traditional fabric divider that restaurants and shops hang outside their doorway to show they are open for business. The choice of material and design of a noren is a subtle indication of a business's class and aesthetic preference. Some businesses even change their noren from season to season. A noren is considered the face of a business, to the extent that growing a business is called "making the noren bigger." Although it is just a sheet of fabric, it also acts as a divider between the inside and outside of a space. A *uchi-noren* is a type of noren hung inside a restaurant to divide the dining area and kitchen. It is also sometimes hung on the inside of the entrance to indicate that first-time customers are not welcome without introduction, a custom particular to some upper-class restaurants.

OSECHI RYORI

おせち料理

New Year's Day food

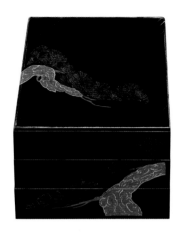

神様と食べる料理
Sharing Food with a Deity

　年中行事と密接に関わる食。和食のそんな文化的、伝統的な側面が、ユネスコの無形文化遺産登録のポイントになりました。一年の始まり、お正月に食べるおせち料理は文字通りその筆頭。

　おせち料理は、黒い漆塗りの箱の中に、幸運への祈りを込めた色や名前、姿の食べ物を詰め合わせたものです。穴の開いたレンコンは将来を見通せるように、エビは腰が曲がるまで長生きできるように、黄金色の栗きんとんは、お金が貯まるように。それらの料理を収めた箱は「めでたさを重ねる」という意味で、重箱になっています。このおせち料理を、元日に家にお迎えする歳神様にお供えし、それを下げて「祝い箸」(*P.102*)を使っていただくことで、神様の力をとりいれようとするのです。お正月には、餅の入ったお雑煮も食べます。餅には稲の霊が宿っていて、食べると生命力が得られると信じられてきました。和食には、家族や友人とだけでなく、神様と共に食べる料理もあるのです。

Washoku, which is registered as an intangible cultural heritage by UNESCO, is a cuisine that has an intricate relationship with traditional events throughout the year. *Osechi ryori*, which is eaten on New Year's Day, is the first and most important event.

Foods with colors, names, and shapes that carry a prayer for good luck are neatly arranged in a layered black lacquer box. Lotus root, with its many holes, stand for helpful foresight. The simmered shrimp represent the hope to live a long life, until one is "bent with age." The golden *kuri kinton* (candied chestnut and sweet potatoes) symbolizes wealth, and the lacquer box that contains everything is layered so that happiness may be manyfold. Osechi ryori is offered to the *Toshigami* ("Year God"), after which it is eaten with *iwaibashi* chopsticks (*P.103*) in the hopes of bringing in some of his powers. *Ozouni*, a soup with *mochi* (rice cake) is also eaten on New Year's Day. It is believed that the rice god dwells in the rice cakes, and eating them is believed to provide vitality. Washoku is enjoyed not only with family and friends, but also with a deity.

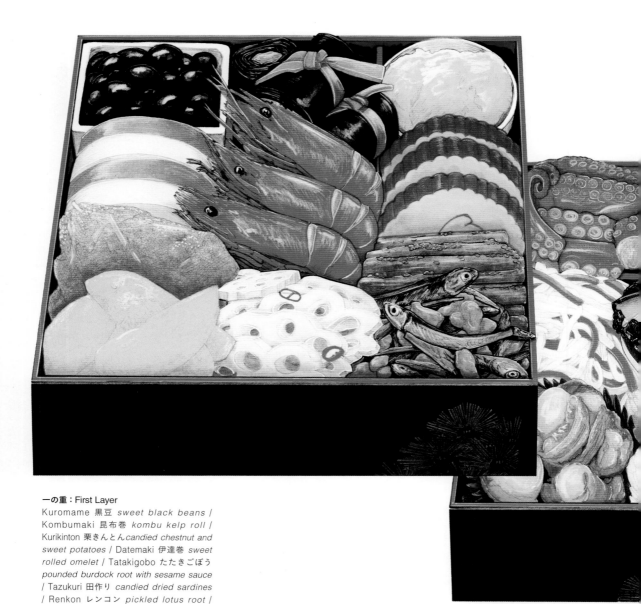

一の重：First Layer

Kuromame 黒豆 *sweet black beans* /
Kombumaki 昆布巻 *kombu kelp roll* /
Kurikinton 栗きんとん *candied chestnut and
sweet potatoes* / Datemaki 伊達巻 *sweet
rolled omelet* / Tatakigobo たたきごぼう
pounded burdock root with sesame sauce
/ Tazukuri 田作り *candied dried sardines*
/ Renkon レンコン *pickled lotus root* /
Kazunoko 数の子 *herring roe* / Tainoko 鯛の
子 *sea bream roe* / Kohaku kamaboko 紅白
かまぼこ *white and red fish cake* / Ebi 海老
simmered shrimp

二の重：Second Layer

Tako タコ *octopus* / Kohada コハダ *gizzard
shad* / Donko どんこ *donko shiitake
mushroom* / Unikurage うにくらげ *sea
urchin and jellyfish* / Yakiburi 焼きブリ *grilled
yellowtail* / Kikkakabu 菊花カブ *pickled
chrysanthemum-shaped turnip* / Hotategai
帆立貝 *scallop* / Kohaku Namasu 紅白なま
す *pickled radish and carrot* / Awabi あわび
abalone

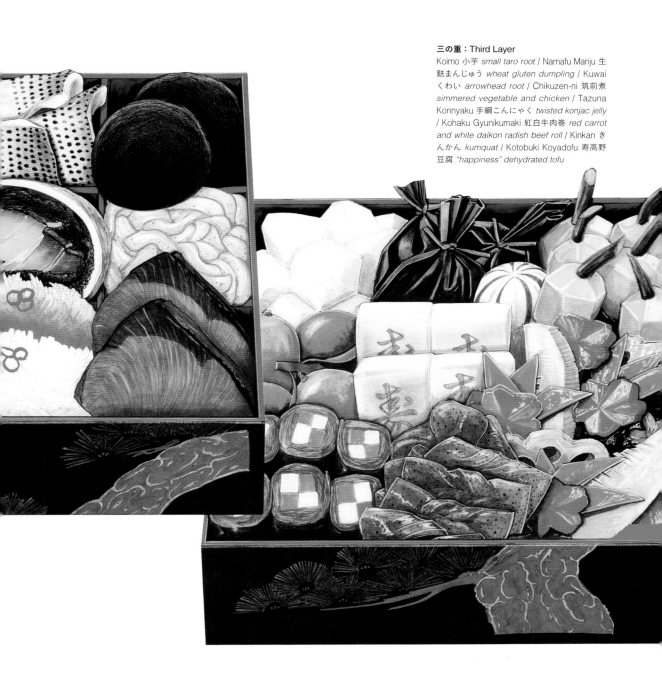

三の重：Third Layer
Koimo 小芋 *small taro root* / Namafu Manju 生
麩まんじゅう *wheat gluten dumpling* / Kuwai
くわい *arrowhead root* / Chikuzen-ni 筑前煮
simmered vegetable and chicken / Tazuna
Konnyaku 手綱こんにゃく *twisted konjac jelly*
/ Kohaku Gyunikumaki 紅白牛肉巻 *red carrot
and white daikon radish beef roll* / Kinkan き
んかん *kumquat* / Kotobuki Koyadofu 寿高野
豆腐 *"happiness" dehydrated tofu*

Sobayu そば湯 *hot soba water* /
Soba そば *buckwheat noodles* /
Sobatsuyu そばつゆ *dipping sauce*
/ Yakumi 薬味 *condiments*

Morisoba
盛りそば
*cold soba noodles
with dipping sauce*

SOBA

そば *buckwheat noodles*

そば通たちが誇る、江戸の粋
A Stylish and Bold Edo Favorite

うどん好きの関西人と、そば好きの関東人。和食の主たる2つの麺には、日本の東西の食の好みが現れています。そばのルーツは、信州（長野県）の郷土料理「そば切り」。江戸時代に、それが現在の東京・江戸に伝わって、屋台から人気が広がりました。以来、そば文化の中心地は東京。そばの名店が集中し、そばの打ち方、味わい方にこだわる「そば通」たちが多くいます。

そばのおいしい食べ方は、ひきたて、打ちたて、ゆでたてを冷水でしめて、一気にたぐる（すする）こと。このテンポの良さが、江戸の人達の粋を愛する心に通じます。「そば通」たちの粋な食べ方は、盛りそばに少しだけつゆをつけて、音を立ててたぐります。この時に、喉ごしとともに喉から鼻に抜けるそばの香りを楽しむのです。食後には、そばをゆでた湯、「そば湯」でつゆを割って飲み、もう一度、そばの香りを味わいます。

It is a widely recognized fact that western Japan loves *udon*, while eastern Japan loves *soba*. One could observe that this reflects the different food preferences of east and west. Today, Tokyo is known as a city bustling with soba connoisseurs and renowned soba restaurants, but in fact, soba as we know it today evolved from *"sobakiri,"* a regional cuisine from Shinshu (Nagano prefecture). It was brought to the city of Edo (now Tokyo) during the Edo period and popularized by street vendors.

Soba is most delicious when made from freshly ground buckwheat, and it is best boiled, chilled, and slurped down vigorously. There is a certain rhythm and speed to soba, and this is what captured the hearts of the chic, urbane people of Edo. Connoisseurs swear by dipping the noodles only slightly in the sauce and slurping them up zealously in order to fully experience the texture and fragrance. *Sobayu*, the boiling water from the soba noodles, is served after the noodles arrive. Add it to the cup of dipping sauce and sip to savor the buckwheat fragrance.

UDON

うどん *udon*

Kitsune Udon

きつねうどん *udon with deep fried tofu*

東西で違うダシの色、全国で違う麺のかたち
The Broths of East and West, and Countless Noodle Types

小麦粉を練って切った白い麺がうどん。1241年に中国から帰国した僧の円爾（えんに）が、製粉技術とうどんの製法を持ち帰り、博多で定着させたと言われています。熱いダシに麺を入れてトッピングをのせるかけうどん、盛りそば（P.44）のように、冷たい麺をつゆにつけて食べる冷やしうどん、どんぶり（P.8）のように具材をのせてつゆに絡ませる「ぶっかけうどん」のような食べ方もあります。

うどんはそばと対照的に西日本、南日本で好まれています。甘く煮た油揚げ（P.82）、甘ぎつねをのせたきつねうどんは大阪発祥。鰹節と昆布が香り高く、透き通った淡い色のダシは、関西人の誇りです。対して、関東方面のダシは醤油の色と香りが強く、黒っぽい色です。関西と関東で違う、うどんダシの濃淡。その分岐点は、安土桃山時代（16世紀）に日本の東西の勢力が戦った関ヶ原（岐阜県）だといわれています。

Udon are white flour noodles which are kneaded and cut into individual strands with a knife. The monk Enni brought back udon along with milling technology from China in 1241, and is said to have popularized it in Hakata, Fukuoka prefecture. Served in hot dashi broth with toppings, chilled and dipped in sauce, or topped with ingredients donburi-style (*P.8*), udon are versatile noodles that can be enjoyed in a variety of ways.

While soba (*P.44*) is the preferred noodle in eastern Japan, udon is much more dominant in western Japan. *Kitsune* udon, which is hot udon served in dashi broth and topped with deep fried *tofu* (*P.82*), is a specialty of Osaka prefecture. The beautifully clear light color of the broth, and its mouth-watering aroma of bonito and kombu kelp is the pride of the Kansai region. Udon broth is very different between western and eastern Japan; it is much darker and has a strong soy sauce aroma in the east. It is said that the dark and light udon broths are bordered at Sekigahara (Gifu prefecture), where eastern and western forces battled during the *Azuchi-Momoyama* period (16th c.).

Udon Varieties
うどんの種類

Ippon Udon
一本うどん *"one string" noodle from Kyoto*

Ise Udon
伊勢うどん *fat and long noodle from Ise, Mie*

Kishimen
きしめん *flat noodle from Aichi*

Sanuki Udon
讃岐うどん *glutenous udon from Kagawa*

Kyo Udon
京うどん *Kyoto udon*

Inaniwa Udon
稲庭うどん *thin and flat udon from Akita*

Shiroishi Umen
白石温麺 *Shiroishi somen noodle from Shiroishi, Miyagi*

　日本全国には、さまざまな形状、食感のうどんがあります。歯が立たないほどの弾力で「喉で食べる」と言われる讃岐うどん、ダシとなじむ柔らかさの京うどん。ユニークなのが、ダシに太麺が1本だけの一本うどん、柔らかい太麺をタレを絡めて食べる伊勢うどんです。平打ちうどんが、名古屋のきしめん。おなじ平打ちでも群馬県桐生市のひもかわうどんは、最大150mmもの幅があります。逆に、細めが秋田県の稲庭うどんです。

　小麦の麺には他に、うどんのほか、細いそうめん (p.94)、うどんとそうめんの中間の冷や麦があります。そうめんは油を使って延ばす製法がうどんとは異なりますが、JAS（日本農林規格）は機械製麺の乾麺を直径0.8～1.3mmがそうめん、1.7mm以上をうどん、と太さで分類しています。宮城県の白石温麺は、冷や麦のようですが、そうめんです。

Himokawa Udon
ひもかわうどん *flat udon from Kiryu, Gumma*

Toppings
うどんトッピング

Tsukimi : Namatamago
月見：生玉子
"moon viewing" : raw egg

Ebi Tempura
エビの天ぷら
shrimp tempura

Amagitsune
甘ぎつね
*sweet simmered
deep fried tofu*

Oboro Kombu
おぼろこんぶ
shaved kombu kelp

Niku
牛肉
*beef seasoned with
soy sauce and sugar*

Wakame
わかめ *wakame seawead*

Tankasu
天かす
tempura flakes

Udon noodles have great regional variety. Kagawa prefecture's *Sanuki* udon is known for a particular elasticity and glutinousness, which lends a pleasant texture not just in the mouth but also going down the throat. *Kyo*-udon is a specialty of Kyoto that emphasizes how well the noodles carry the dashi flavor. Mie prefecture's *Ise* udon are thick noodles with very little bounce that are seasoned with sauce. There are also a variety of flat udon noodles, including *kishimen* from Nagoya, Aichi prefecture. *Himokawa* udon from Kiryu, Gunma prefecture, is famously wide, ranging from 5cm to 15cm in breadth.

Somen (*P.94*) on the other hand, are very thin flour noodles. Although unlike udon, they are stretched with the help of oil, the JAS (Japanese Agricultural Standards) define mechanically manufactured round dry noodles between 0.8~1.3mm thick as somen, and noodles thicker than 1.7mm as udon. There is also *hiyamugi*, a medium width noodle between somen and udon known for a softer texture. Many regional varieties border these noodle types; *Inaniwa* udon from Akita prefecture is closer in texture to hiyamugi, while *Shiroishi umen* from Shiroishi city, Miyagi prefecture, is a thicker somen that is visually closer to hiyamugi.

Shoyu Ramen
醤油ラーメン
soy sauce ramen

RAMEN
ラーメン *ramen*

Nitamago
煮卵
marinated egg

Horenso
ホウレンソウ
spinach

Negi
ネギ
scallion

Chashu
チャーシュー
braised pork

Menma
メンマ
*fermented
bamboo shoot*

Naruto
なると
naruto fish cake

Men
麺 *noodles*

Supu
スープ *soup*

Tare
タレ
seasoning sauce

地元の星も、ミシュランの星も。世界に輝く国民食
A National Food Shining Abroad with Local and Michelin Stars

ラーメンのルーツは中国の麺料理で、「中華そば」(P.36)などと呼ばれることもありました。ラーメンという呼び名が定着したのは、1958年に安藤百福が発明し、2017年には世界中で1001億食以上が消費される人気となったインスタントラーメンがきっかけでした。日本の大衆食だったラーメンは海外進出もさかんになり、個性や味の追求も激化。2015年にはラーメン店が初めてミシュランの星を獲得しました。ラーメンの味には、醤油、味噌、塩、豚骨などがあります。スープは野菜、鶏がら、昆布、煮干しなどを煮込んだダシに、味付けのタレを調合してつくります。麺の太さや食感は千差万別あり、スープとの最高の相性を求めて自家製麺するシェフもいます。世界に2つと同じ味がないのが、ファンを熱狂させるラーメンの魅力。地元密着のご当地ラーメンあり、マスコミを賑わす新進気鋭のイノベーティブなラーメンあり。一杯で、地域色もシェフたちの熱いクラフトマンシップも味わえます。

Ramen has its roots in Chinese noodle dishes and was thus initially referred to as *"chuka soba,"* (*P.36*) meaning "Chinese noodles." The term "ramen" became popularized in 1958, thanks to the instant ramen, which was invented by entrepreneur and founder of Nisshin Foods, Momofuku Ando. The instant ramen continues to garner global popularity ever since. Ramen earned its first Michelin star in 2015, and 100.1 billion instant ramen noodles were consumed worldwide in 2017 alone. Soy sauce, miso, salt, and pork bone broth are some of the classic flavors, but we are witnessing an ever-intensifying pursuit of individuality and flavor, especially now that ramen has entered the global food scene. Ramen broth is usually a vegetable, chicken, kelp, or dried sardine stock, seasoned with a thick sauce. The noodles can vary infinitely in thickness and texture, and many ramen chefs develop their own noodles to best match their signature soups. Whether it be local ramen featuring regional customs and ingredients, or an inventive, new-wave ramen, each bowl brings unique regional characteristics and passionate craftsmanship.

Nitamago

煮卵

marinated eggs

半熟のゆで卵を醤油で味付け。「味玉」とも呼ばれる

Soft-boiled egg marinated with soy sauce-based seasoning. Also called ajitama.

Menma

メンマ

fermented bamboo shoot

マチクを乳酸発酵させた、中国南部や台湾の食品。日本でラー"メン"の上の"マ"チク、メンマと命名された

A fermented food initially from Southern China and Taiwan made with machiku bamboo shoots. Its Japanese name "menma" is a hybrid of the two words "ramen" and "machiku."

Negi

ネギ *scallion*

白ネギは関東、青ネギは関西好み

White scallion is preferred in the Kanto (eastern) region and green scallion in the Kansai (western) region.

Naruto

なると *naruto fish cake*

渦の模様があるカマボコ。鳴門海峡のうず潮をかたどっている

Naruto is a fish cake with a spiral pattern that represents the Naruto whirlpools in the Naruto Strait.

Horenso

ホウレンソウ *spinach*

野菜のトッピングにはモヤシやキクラゲなどのほか、アクセントに高菜やキムチなど辛い漬物も

Bean sprouts, seaweed, and wood ear mushroom are also common vegetable toppings. Pickles such as takana and kimchi are also sometimes added as an accent.

Chashu

チャーシュー

braised pork

中国の焼き豚と違って、脂身のある豚の三枚肉を、醤油味で柔らかく煮たもの。店のアイデンティティとも言える大切なトッピング

Chashu is the Japanese version of char siu or Chinese-style braised pork. Unlike the Chinese version, the rich pork belly meat is simmered with soy sauce until tender. An important topping that carries the identity of a ramen restaurant.

Supu

スープ *soup*

豚骨、鶏ガラ、煮干し、昆布 (P.84)、野菜などからとったダシに、醤油や味噌 (P.108) ベースのタレを加える

Miso (P.108) or soy-based sauce is added to pork bone, chicken bone, dried sardine, kombu kelp(P.84), or vegetable broth.

Men

麺 *noodles*

太麺、細麺、縮れ麺、ストレート麺など、形状もテクスチャーもいろいろ。客の好みの食感を、ゆで加減で調整する店もある

Ramen noodles can vary anywhere between thick and thin, curly and straight. Some restaurants boil to customers' texture preferences.

Ramen Variations
ラーメンのいろいろ

Hakata Tonkotsu Ramen
博多豚骨ラーメン
Hakata-style
pork bone broth ramen

Tantanmen
担々麺
tantan noodle

　ラーメン王国・日本には、47都道府県すべてに名物ラーメンがあり、そこでしか食べられない特色ある味を求めて、ラーメンを目当てにしたフードツーリズムも盛んです。日本三大ラーメンと言われるのが、北海道・札幌発祥の味噌ラーメン、白く濃厚なスープの博多豚骨ラーメン、醤油味のスープに柔らかい麺の福島県・喜多方ラーメン。さらに、ラーメンのバリエーションは未体験の味を求めて拡大し続けています。ゴマ風味の辛く濃厚なスープが人気を呼び、近年新たに定着したのが中国の四川料理を日本風にアレンジした担々麺。まぜ麺／つけ麺は、盛りそば（P.44）のように、水でしめた麺を濃いめのタレでいただく、麺を主役にした新スタイル。冷やし中華は、日本の中華料理店の夏限定のメニュー。玉子焼きやハムをのせた見た目は、ぶっかけうどん（P.46）に似ていますが、甘酸っぱいタレは酢の物（P.76）のような爽やかな味わい。日本人は、蒸し暑い季節にもラーメンをあきらめません。

Hiyashi Chuka
冷やし中華
Chinese-style cold ramen

Mazemen
Tsukemen
まぜ麺 / つけ麺
brothless ramen &
dipping ramen

With each of its 47 prefectures full of local specialty ramen, Japan is a kingdom of ramen, where many travel to discover new flavors. The three major ramens are said to be the Sapporo-born miso ramen, the Hakata pork bone broth ramen which has a rich, white broth, and the Fukushima-born *Kitakata* ramen, which features a soy sauce-based broth and soft noodles. However, new variations are constantly entering the scene. The *tantanmen* which features a rich, spicy, sesame-flavored soup, is a relatively new favorite inspired by *dandan* noodles, a dish from Sichuan, China. *Mazemen* and *tsukemen*, or broth-less ramen and dipping ramen, are also popular innovations that highlight the noodles. Similar to *morisoba* (*P.44*), the boiled noodles are rinsed in cold water and dipped in or mixed with a thick sauce. Another variation suitable for the summer is *hiyashi chuka*, or Chinese-style cold ramen. Topped with shredded egg crepes and ham, the dish is visually similar to donburi-style *bukkake* udon (*P.46*), but the sweet and tart sauce is closer to *sunomono* (*P.76*) in flavor. Even during the hot and humid summers, the Japanese do not give up their ramen.

OKONOMIYAKI

お好み焼き *savory pancake*

Hirosima Okonomiyaki

広島風お好み焼き

Hiroshima-style okonomiyaki

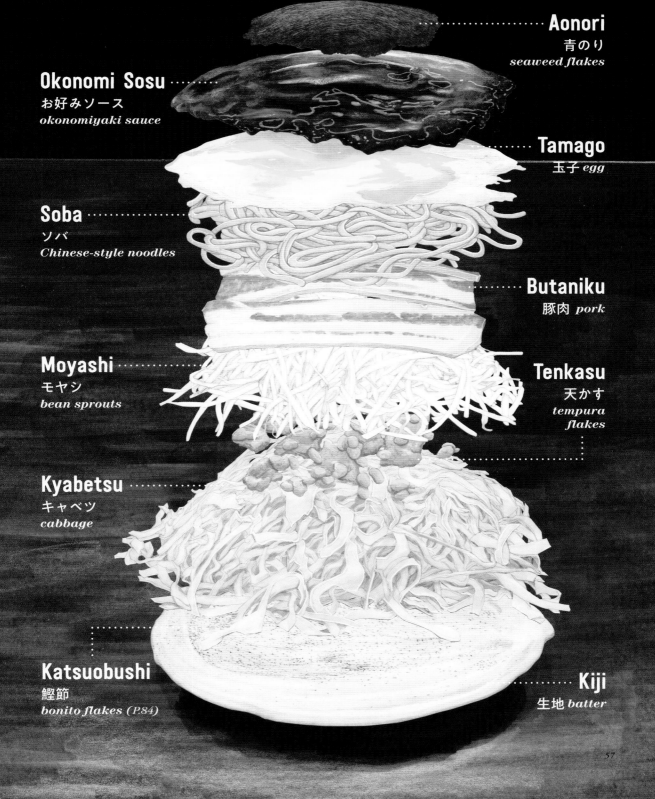

Aonori
青のり
seaweed flakes

Okonomi Sosu
お好みソース
okonomiyaki sauce

Tamago
玉子 *egg*

Soba
ソバ
Chinese-style noodles

Butaniku
豚肉 *pork*

Moyashi
モヤシ
bean sprouts

Tenkasu
天かす
tempura flakes

Kyabetsu
キャベツ
cabbage

Katsuobushi
鰹節
bonito flakes (P.84)

Kiji
生地 *batter*

57

ルーツは大道芸？ 遊び心が香ばしい、鉄板粉ものスナック
The Iron Griddle Snack that Evolved from Street Performance

水で薄く溶いた小麦粉を鉄板に丸く広げ、その上にキャベツや肉を山のように盛って、鮮やかなコテさばきで裏返す広島風お好み焼き。これに対し、具材を混ぜてから焼くのが大阪風お好み焼きです。甘いお好みソースには、中東産のドライフルーツ、デーツが入っています。小麦粉を使った鉄板焼きスナックには、キャベツの代わりにネギを使ったネギ焼き、鉄板の丸いくぼみで、タコ入りの生地を焼くタコ焼きがあります。お好み焼きの起源は諸説ありますが、面白いのが、小麦粉の生地で鉄板の上に文字や動物の姿をかたどって駄菓子を焼くという江戸時代の大道芸が明治末期にパロディ料理となり、そこに当時流行っていた西洋料理のソースをかけて、現在のお好み焼きに発展したという説です。ソースをかけて焼く焼きそばは、中国料理の炒麺のパロディ。これを、大阪風お好み焼きにのせて焼いたのがモダン焼きで、発祥は神戸だと言われます。お好み焼きは路上に生まれ、庶民の遊び心が育てたソウルフードです。

Osaka Okonomiyaki
大阪風お好み焼き
Osaka-style okonomiyaki

Negiyaki
ネギ焼き
green scallion okonomiyaki

The Hiroshima-style *okonomiyaki* is made with a thin flour batter, which is spread on an iron griddle, topped with a mountain of cabbage and meat, and skillfully flipped at the end. Contrastly, the Osaka-style okonomiyaki is made with a batter with the ingredients mixed in prior to grilling. Both are topped with okonomiyaki sauce, which has a sweet flavor because of a surprising ingredient; dates, the Middle Eastern dried fruit. There are many different variations of flour batter snacks that are prepared on an iron griddle, such as the *negiyaki*, which is made with scallions instead of cabbage, or *takoyaki* octopus balls, which is made with octopus-filled batter grilled into spheres in a cast iron mold. Although there are various hypotheses as to how the okonomiyaki was born, one interesting theory is that its predecessor was a popular performative Edo-period snack made by grilling a flour batter in letter or animal shapes. This evolved into the okonomiyaki at the end of the Meiji period when people started eating them with Japanese Worcestershire sauce, which was the fad at the time. *Yakisoba* noodles, which are also prepared on an iron griddle and seasoned with Japanese Worcestershire sauce, is a Japanese take on the Chinese dish chow mein. Okonomiyaki is a beloved comfort food born on the streets and popularized by the playful spirit of everyday working people.

Yakisoba
焼きそば
pan fried noodles

Takoyaki
タコ焼き
octopus balls

ODEN

おでん *oden stew*

1. Ganmodoki がんもどき *deep fried tofu ball* 2. Daikon 大根 *daikon radish* 3. Tamago 玉子 *boiled egg* 4. Chikuwabu ちくわぶ *"bamboo ring" wheat gluten* 5. Gobomaki ゴボウ巻 *fish cake with burdock root* 6. Hiraten 平天 *deep fried flat fish cake* 7. Mochi-kinchaku もち巾着 *rice cake wrapped in deep fried tofu* 8. Tofu 豆腐 *tofu* 9. Hanpen はんぺん *triangular fish cake with mountain yam* 10. Shirataki しらたき *konjac jelly noodle* 11. Konnyaku コンニャク *konjac jelly* 12. Atsuage 厚揚げ *thick deep fried tofu* 13. Chikuwa ちくわ *"bamboo ring" fish cake* 14. Jagaimo じゃがいも *potato* 15. Roru Kyabetsu ロールキャベツ *cabbage roll* 16. Suji すじ *beef tendon*

ユニークな具材の共演。主役はたっぷりしみ込んだダシ
Unique Ingredients Infused with Dashi Broth, the Star of the Show

　温かいダシに浸かったおでんは、庶民の冬の味覚。家庭でも居酒屋（P.110）でも人気です。おでんは英語で説明するのがちょっと難しいメニューです。"hodge-podge(ごった煮) "と説明されたり、"日本版ポトフ"ともいわれますが、調理法が大きく違います。ポトフが肉や野菜を煮込んだスープであるのに対して、おでんはダシの味を具材に含ませる料理です。大根は下ゆでし、コンニャクには隠し包丁を入れたりして、具材にダシがよくしみ込むように下ごしらえがされています。ちくわやはんぺん、ゴボウ巻などの練り物も、西欧人にはミステリアスな食材。これらはタラなど白身の魚をすり身にして、揚げたり蒸した"fish cake"です。日本は練り物の種類が豊富で、魚肉ソーセージやカニかまぼこのような、独自の練り物バリエーションを誇ります。

　Simmered in dashi broth, *oden* is a winter favorite enjoyed in the home or at *izakaya* (*P.110*), but it is a rather tricky dish to explain in English. Although sometimes called "hodge-podge" or "Japanese pot-au-feu," neither term is quite accurate, because the idea of oden is to infuse the ingredients with the flavor of dashi. Some ingredients are prepared in specific ways to help soak up the flavor; the daikon radish for instance is pre-boiled, and the konjac jelly is scored beforehand. Other staple oden ingredients include *nerimono* such as *chikuwa*, *hanpen*, and *gobomaki*. Perhaps mysterious to the Western eye, nerimono are fish cakes made from white fish such as cod, which are ground into a smooth paste and steamed or fried. There are many variations of nerimono in Japan, including modern twists like fish sausage or *kanikama* imitation crab.

YAKITORI

焼き鳥 *skewered chicken*

一羽の鶏から、驚きの20種以上の串メニュー

串に刺した鶏肉を焼いて、塩やタレで食べる。鶏肉の料理は世界にたくさんありますが、焼き鳥は、内臓も含め20種類以上（50種類という料理人もいる）もの部位の味や食感が楽しめるという、驚くべき料理です。かつては大衆的な屋台や立ち飲み屋での酒のつまみでしたが、今では老若男女が楽しめる、居酒屋（P.110）スタイルの店が海外にも増えています。

味にこだわる専門店では、地鶏と呼ばれる平飼いの在来種や、地方特産の銘柄鶏を使い、うちわで風を送ることで火力を調整しながら、炭で焼いています。焼き鳥に限らず、和食では、焼き物はこの炭焼きがもっとも美味しいとされます。

焼き鳥は、庶民が安く手に入る鶏肉や内臓肉をおいしく食べるために知恵を絞った料理です。それゆえ、土地によって豊かなバリエーションがあります。北海道美唄市の「もつ串」は、鶏のさまざまな内臓を一本の串に刺して焼きます。愛媛県の「今治焼き」は、串に刺さずに鉄板で焼きます。なぜか牛肉や豚肉、馬肉を「焼き鳥」と呼ぶ地域もあります。

One Bird, Over 20 Skewer Types

Yakitori, which literally translates to "grilled chicken," is a simple dish of skewered chicken seasoned with salt or a savory sauce. It is an amazing dish for sampling the various flavors and textures of the over 20 different parts (some restaurants serve 50) that one chicken lends, including the internal organs. Although it was initially more of a bar food served at standing bars or street vendors, today it is mostly enjoyed at izakaya-style restaurants (*P.110*) and is even gaining popularity overseas.

At specialty yakitori restaurants, a local breed of free-range chicken called *jidori* or local brand chicken are grilled over a charcoal fire. A hand-held fan is used to adjust the heat. In Japan, charcoal grilling is considered a highly elevated cooking method.

Yakitori is a clever dish that the working class devised as a way to enjoy inexpensive chicken meat and organ parts. There are various local styles of yakitori, such as the *motsugushi* or "organ skewer" of Bibai city, Hokkaido, which is an assortment of organ pieces on one skewer. Another example is the *imabariyaki* of Aichi prefecture, which is grilled on an iron griddle instead of on a skewer. In some parts of Japan, beef, pork, and horse skewers are referred to as "yakitori" as well.

NABE

鍋 *hot pot*

Chanko Nabe
ちゃんこ鍋 *sumo stable hot pot*

お腹も絆も温める、冬の食卓の横綱
Warming Up and Strengthening Bonds with the Champion of Winter Dishes

　大きな鍋で、肉、魚、魚介や野菜を煮るから「鍋」。最高にシンプルな料理です。料理する人が食べる人を兼ね、調理と食事を同時進行させながら、皆が一緒につつき合って食べる。家族や職場の仲間とコミュニケーションを生み出す鍋は、寒い季節に、お腹も心も温めてくれます。相撲部屋に住み込んで稽古する力士たちも、ちゃんこ鍋を食べて師弟や仲間との絆を深めます。相撲では、土俵に手がつくと負けなので、手（前足）を地につけた4本脚の動物は縁起が悪いとされ、鍋の具材には鶏肉が好まれます。引退した力士が経営するちゃんこ鍋店は、意外なことに、女性客にも人気です。野菜をたっぷりとれる鍋は、実はダイエットの味方なのです。

　共食の楽しさと具材の滋味を味わえるのが鍋の良さですが、和食の多様化を反映するかのように、最近ではスーパーマーケットにキムチ味、トマト味、カレー味などのインスタント鍋スープが登場し、家庭の鍋に無国籍な味が進出。一人で食べる小さいサイズの鍋の普及もあり、鍋の風景も変化しています。

Nabe, which literally means "pot," is a very simple one-pot dish, where meat, seafood, and vegetables are simmered together in a large pot. Everyone is involved in the cooking and eating, which happens. It is a communal dish that encourages communication. *Chanko nabe* is a type of nabe *sumo* wrestlers in training eat to help strengthen all bonds within the sumo stable. Because a sumo wrester loses a match by touching the ground with his hands, four-legged livestock that use their "hands" to walk are considered bad luck. Thus, the chanko nabe features chicken, the sumo wrestler's preferred meat. Being a healthy, balanced dish packed with nutritious vegetables and protein, chanko nabe restaurants run by retired wrestlers are especially popular among health-conscious women.

The communal aspect and the flavors of the ingredients themselves are what make nabe special, but today, various instant nabe broths in *kimchi*, tomato, curry, and other flavors are available in supermarkets, and one-person pots are on the rise; it seems even the nabe scene is changing with the times.

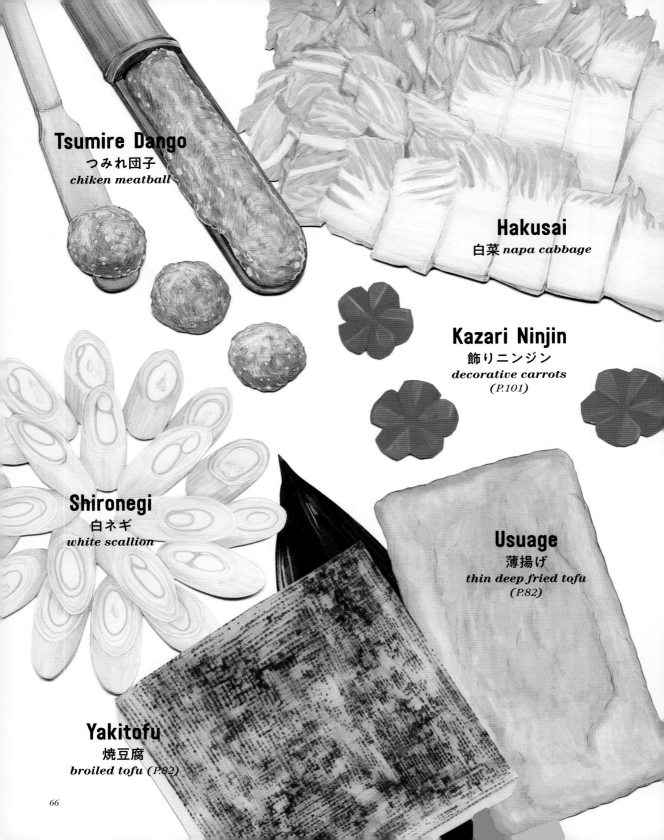

Tsumire Dango
つみれ団子
chiken meatball

Hakusai
白菜 *napa cabbage*

Kazari Ninjin
飾りニンジン
decorative carrots
(P.101)

Shironegi
白ネギ
white scallion

Usuage
薄揚げ
thin deep fried tofu
(P.82)

Yakitofu
焼豆腐
broiled tofu (P.82)

Chanko Nabe Ingredients
ちゃんこ鍋の具材

Shiitake
シイタケ
shiitake mushroom

Enokidake
エノキダケ
enoki mushroom

Shungiku
春菊
chrysanthemum greens

Soppu Dashi
そっぷダシ
chicken broth

Shirataki
しらたき
konjac jelly noodle

67

Chirinabe Variations
ちり鍋のいろいろ

Yudofu
湯豆腐
tofu hot pot

Tecchiri
てっちり
*blowfish
hot pot*

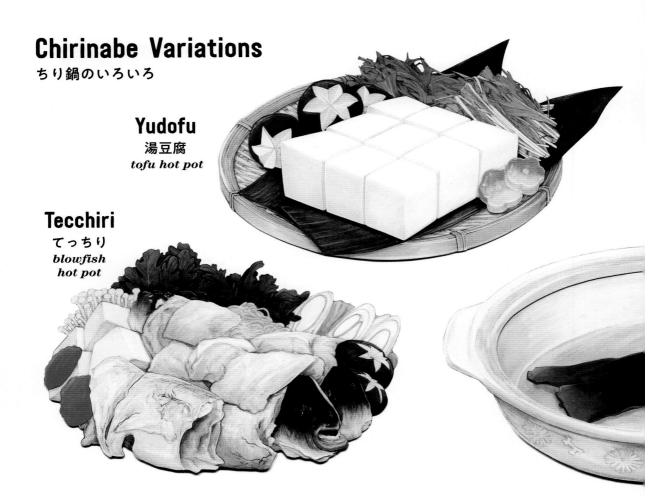

鍋天国、日本。各地のご当地鍋には、北海道の鮭の石狩鍋、茨城のアンコウ鍋、東京のどじょう鍋、福岡のもつ鍋、北海道、山陰、北陸地方のカニ鍋‥‥と、数限りなくあり、その郷土色が旅人の心を駆り立てます。鍋は冬のフードツーリズムの花型です。魚醤（ぎょしょう）スープのしょっつる鍋や、味噌味で煮込む牡蠣の土手鍋、猪のぼたん鍋など、スープに特徴のある鍋もありますが、具材をシンプルに味わえるのが「ちり鍋」です。ふぐ、カニ、伊勢海老、豆腐などを、味付けのない昆布ダシであっさりと

煮て、醤油、酢に柚子やカボスなどの柑橘果汁を合わせた「ポン酢」と大根おろし、ネギなどの薬味を添えていただきます。最後に、具材のおいしさが凝縮されたスープに、うどんやご飯を入れて食べます。"シメ"とよばれる、鍋のもう一つの楽しみです。

ちり鍋の"ちり"は、魚がちりちりと縮む様子から名付けられたという説があります。「しゃぶしゃぶ鍋」は、肉を熱いダシにくぐらせる食べ方から。「はりはり鍋」は水菜の歯ごたえから名づけられました。

Kani-nabe
カニ鍋
crab hot pot

Burishabu
ぶりしゃぶ
*yellowtail
shabu shabu*

Kombu Dashi
昆布ダシ
kelp-flavored broth

Salmon *Ishikari* nabe from Hokkaido, pond loach *dojyo* nabe from Tokyo, offal *motsu* nabe from Fukuoka, and crab *kani* nabe from northern and coastal regions: these are some of the countless local specialty hot pots found all over Japan. Because nabe is an excellent way to enjoy local ingredients in quantity, it is a celebrated dish, especially in the world of food tourism. Some nabe feature unique soups, like *shottsuru* nabe which is flavored with Japanese fish sauce, *dote* nabe which is an oyster nabe simmered with miso, and *botan* nabe which is wild boar hot pot. *Chiri* nabe on the other hand, is made with kombu kelp broth—the ultimate simple soup. Ingredients

such as blowfish, crab, Japanese spiny lobster, tofu, and vegetables are simmered in the mild kelp broth and dipped in *ponzu*—a combination of soy sauce, vinegar, and *yuzu*, *kabosu*, or other citrus juice—along with condiments such as grated daikon radish and scallions. The emphasis here is on the flavors of the ingredients themselves, which the simple seasonings enhance. At the end of the meal, rice or udon is added to the soup, which has absorbed the goodness of all the ingredients. Called "*shime*," which translates to "closing" and applies to a carb-based dish that concludes a long meal, this is another highlight of nabe.

Sukiyaki
すき焼き *beef pot*

Shirataki
しらたき
konjac jelly noodle

Fu 麩
wheat gluten

Shironegi
白ネギ
white scallion

日本を「開化」させた
特別なごちそう

　鍋の一種ではあるけれど、すき"焼き"と呼ばれるのは、最初に熱した鉄鍋に薄切りの牛肉を焼くから。それを砂糖と醤油、または醤油を砂糖、みりん (P.108)などで調味した「わりした」と野菜で煮て、溶いた生卵にくぐらせて食べます。

　明治4年 (1871)に肉食禁止令が解かれ、西洋の食文化である牛肉を和風の甘い醤油味で食べさせる「肉鍋」の店は文明開化の象徴となり「肉鍋食わぬ奴は、開けぬ奴」という流行語まで生まれました。この肉鍋から発展したすき焼きは、今も家庭のご馳走。精肉店では、薄くスライスされた高級な赤身の牛肉が「すき焼き用肉」として販売され、贈答にも用いられます。

Shungiku
春菊
chrysanthemum greens

Sukiyaki yo Niku
すき焼き用肉
sukiyaki beef

Yakitofu
焼き豆腐
broiled tofu (P.82)

Shiitake
シイタケ *shiitake mushroom*

A Special Treat that Propelled Japan's Modernization

Although *sukiyaki* is a type of hot pot that is cooked in an iron pot, it is prepared slightly differently from the standard nabe, as is suggested in the name. The "yaki" in sukiyaki, which means "stir-fried" or "broiled," refers to the thinly sliced beef that is stir-fried in the beginning. Once the beef is cooked through, vegetables are added to the pot and simmered with a sauce called "*warishita*" which is a combination of soy sauce, sugar, and mirin *(P.108)*. Freshly beat raw egg is used as a dipping sauce.

The history of sukiyaki is very much tied to the history of beef in Japan, which only began when the meat ban was lifted in the 4th year of the Meiji period (1871). Beef was considered the epitome of Western cuisine, and restaurants that served "beef nabe" simmered in sweet soy sauce became a symbol of modernization, so much so that "he who does not eat beef nabe cannot be civilized" was a popular saying at the time. Eventually, the "beef nabe" evolved into sukiyaki as we know it today. Considered a special treat, it is often cooked with high quality beef. Thinly sliced high-grade "sukiyaki beef" is sold at butcher shops, and even presented as gifts.

Enokidake
エノキダケ
enoki mushroom

BENTO

弁当 *bento*

Shiumai Bento

シウマイ弁当
steamed dumpling bento

今や、世界から羨望される日本の「片付け」センス。それが和食にあらわれたのが弁当です。蓋を開けた時、箱に詰め合わされたおかずの色彩と味のバランスには、ときめきを禁じえません。学校や職場での昼食には、多くの人が手作りや、コンビニや飲食店でテイクアウトした弁当を食べています。手早く食べられる便利な携帯食としての弁当の歴史は古く、記録に残る最古の弁当は、奈良時代（8世紀）の干し飯でした。

いつもと違う場所で食べる弁当で、非日常を味わうこともあります。安土桃山時代（16世紀）には、上流階級の人達が蒔絵漆器の豪華な弁当箱を提げて、野外での花見や茶会を催しました。江戸時代の歌舞伎見物の観客が幕間に食べたのが、現在、弁当の定番となっている幕の内です。列車での旅の楽しみは何と言っても「駅弁」。観光地の駅では、その地を象徴する食材を盛り込んだ弁当が売られています。横浜ではシウマイ弁当、静岡では鰻弁当、神戸ではビーフステーキ弁当。車窓の景色とともに食べる駅弁に、旅情が高まります。

思わずときめく、おかずの収納センス
The Splendidly Tidy Art of Assorting Food in a Box

Open a bento box to find a beautiful assortment of rice and sides. One can sense the Japanese mentality of tidying up in the way a balanced variety of food is arranged in a limited space. In Japan, it is common to bring a homemade or store-bought bento for lunch to school or to the workplace. In fact, the history of bento as a quick and portable meal reaches back many centuries. The oldest bento known in Japanese history is *hoshiii* (dried rice) from the Nara period (8th c.), which was carried around and rehydrated to eat.

Being portable, bento can be a great way to enjoy the experience of eating outdoors or in new settings. It is also extremely versatile, which means there are many different types of bento depending on the occasion or setting. During the Azuchi-Momoyama period (16th c.) for example, the upper-class enjoyed exquisite meals arranged in elaborate lacquerware bento boxes at flower viewing picnics and outdoor tea ceremonies. The *makunouchi* bento, which was invented during the Edo period as an intermission meal for *kabuki* theaters, is an example of a classic bento still popular today. *Ekiben* are specialty bentos packed with local ingredients that are sold at major train stations, and are arguably the best part of a train trip. Some famous ekiben include Yokohama's *shiumai* Bento, Shizuoka's eel bento, and Kobe's beefsteak bento. Enjoyed on the train in tandem with the changing scenery, ekiben are beloved items that enhance the travel experience.

Contents of Shiumai Bento
シウマイ弁当の中身

Kyogi
経木
wooden bento box

Baran
バラン
decorative divider (P.96)

Shoyu
醤油
soy sauce

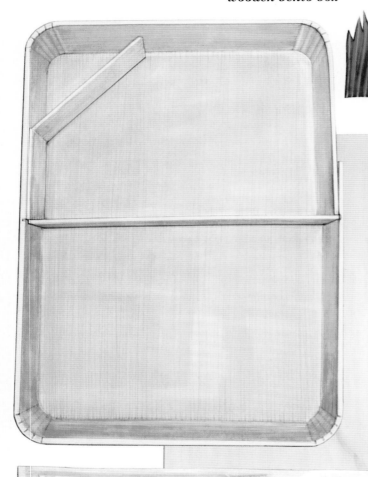

Karashi
辛子
mustard

Waribashi & Otefuki
割り箸、お手拭き
disposable chopsticks and hand wipe

Kirikombu & Sengiri Shouga
切り昆布＆千切り生姜
chopped kombu and ginger

Tamagoyaki
玉子焼き
omelet

Maguro-no-dukeyaki
鮪の漬け焼
broiled marinated tuna

Tori-no-karaage
鶏の唐揚げ
fried chicken

Kamaboko
蒲鉾
fish cake

Takenoko-ni
筍煮
simmered bamboo shoot

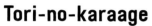

Anzu
あんず
simmered apricot

Koume
小梅
salted plum

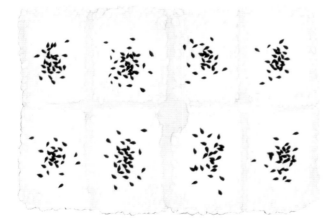

Tawaragata Gohan (kurogoma)
俵型ご飯（黒胡麻）
rice bale-shaped rice with black sesame

Mukashinagara-no Shiumai
昔ながらのシウマイ
classic steamed dumplings

Ohitashi :

Horenso no Ohitashi
ほうれん草のおひたし
marinated spinach

Aemono :

Kinome-ae
木の芽和え
*bamboo shoot with
white miso and kinome
dressing*

Sunomono :

Uzaku
うざく
*vinegared cucumber
and grilled eel*

KOBACHI

小鉢 *side dishes*

フレッシュな和のソース
The Fresh Flavors of Japanese Marinades and Dressings

フランス料理はソースの豊富さを誇りますが、実は和食もソースを多用します。醤油、味噌、酢をベースに、フレーバーを加えた和のソース「かけ酢」「和え衣」を駆使する料理が、酢の物や、和え物です。これらの和のソースは、西洋料理のように煮詰めて素材の味を覆い隠すことをせず、生のハーブや香辛料、かんきつ果汁のフレッシュな香りで素材の風味を引き立てます。塩もみしたキュウリと鰻の蒲焼（P.26）をショウガ酢で和える酢の物「うざく」は、心地よい酸味が暑い夏に向く一品。木の芽の和え衣で若いタケノコ（P.94）を和えた「木の芽和え」は、ほろ苦さに春を感じさせる小鉢料理。ゆでた野菜をダシ醤油に浸した「おひたし」は、英語の和食の解説本では "日本のサラダ" と紹介されることもあります。定食（P.28）や弁当（P.72）にも欠かせない、野菜のサイドディッシュです。

French cuisine is known for its many sauces, but marinades and sauces are also surprisingly important in Japanese cuisine. Sunomono (vinegared dishes) and *aemono* (dressed dishes) are side dishes seasoned with soy sauce, miso, or vinegar-based "*kakesu*" (drizzling vinegar) or "*aegoromo*" (dressing). Japanese marinades are characterized by fresh herbs, spices, and fragrant citruses that enhance the flavor of the ingredients themselves, which some Western sauces tend to mask. *Uzaku* is a sunomono dish with salted sliced cucumbers and chopped grilled eel (*P.26*), seasoned with ginger vinegar. Its pleasant acidity makes it a perfect summer dish. *Kinome-ae* is a side dish with bamboo shoots (*P.94*) dressed in a fresh sauce made with *kinome* (Japanese pepper leaves), an herb that represents the spring. *Ohitashi*, sometimes called "the Japanese salad" in Western contexts, are boiled vegetables marinated in soy sauce and dashi broth. These bright and simple vegetable-centric sides complete the Japanese meal and are essential to teishoku (*P.28*) and bento (*P.72*).

Tai Kabutoni
鯛かぶと煮
*simmered
red sea bream head*

Nikujaga
肉じゃが
*simmered
beef and potatoes*

Takiawase
炊き合わせ
*assorted
simmered foods*

NIMONO

煮物 *simmered dishes*

繊細さも豪快さも。「煮る」料理法いろいろ
The Delicate and Bold Japanese Simmered Foods

　和食の煮物は、手法や調味法で30種類以上あるといわれます。「炊き合わせ」は、素材の色と風味を生かして別々に調理した煮物を、器の中に盛り込んだもの。会席料理店でこうした繊細な煮物を担当するのは、"煮方"と呼ばれる最高の料理人です。根菜や肉などに醤油で濃い味をつける煮しめは、家庭料理。保存性があり、弁当（P.72）や、おせち料理（P.41）にも重宝されます。醤油とみりん（P.108）でコクと照りを出して煮る煮魚は、おかずにも、日本酒のアテにも人気。鯛の頭を煮た「かぶと煮」は、身を外したあとのアラを煮たもので、眼とその周りの柔らかい肉は、魚好きの大好物です。

　どこの国にも「おふくろの味」がありますが、和食でそれを代表するのは、牛肉をじゃがいも、ニンジン、タマネギと煮た「肉じゃが」です。明治時代にイギリスのシチューを参考にして軍隊の食事に導入されたものといわれ、軍港のあった京都府舞鶴市と広島県呉市が「肉じゃが発祥の地」に名乗りをあげています。兵士に力をつけるための煮物が、家族思いのおふくろの味になりました。

There are said to be over 30 different types of *nimono* or simmered dishes in Japanese cuisine, all seasoned and cooked differently. The most sophisticated type of nimono is the *takiawase*, in which each ingredient is cooked separately to preserve the individual colors and flavors. *Nishime* is a more casual dish of simmered root vegetables and meat seasoned generously with soy sauce. It has a longer shelf life, which makes it an ideal component of bento (*P.72*) as well as traditional New Year's Day food (*P.41*). *Nizakana* or simmered fish is a popular main dish seasoned with soy sauce and mirin (*P.108*), which deepens the flavor and creates an appealing glaze. *Kabuto-ni* which translates to "simmered helmet" is the simmered head and other leftover parts of sea bream after the meat is removed. The eyes and delicate meat around them is the fish lover's favorite.

Every country has its flavors of home. *Niku-jaga* or "beef and potatoes" simmered with carrot and onion, is a classic example. Interestingly, this dish is said to have been inspired by British stew, and created by chefs of the Imperial Japanese Navy during the Meiji period. The military port cities of Maizuru (Kyoto) and Kure (Hiroshima) both credit themselves as its originator. Today, it is synonymous with mom's home cooking.

What is This?
2

箱に入った会席料理・松花堂弁当
Kaiseki Ryori in a Box?

日本料理店の昼食メニューに、漆塗りの箱や籠に刺身や天ぷらなどを盛り込んだ「お弁当」があります。この"持ち運ばない弁当"のルーツは、昭和初期に「吉兆」の湯木貞一 (*P.38*) が、お茶会の軽食として考案した松花堂弁当です。箱に仕切りを設け、中に小さな器を入れることで、汁気の多い料理や、温かい料理と冷たい料理を同時に盛り込めるように工夫されています。会席料理のコースの内容を少しずつ味わうことができる、お手軽なメニューといえるでしょう。

Traditional Japanese restaurants often offer "bentos" on their lunch menus; a beautiful assortment of kaiseki dishes (*P.38*) such as sashimi or tempura, served in a lacquer or woven box. This style of serving bento within a restaurant setting was devised by Yuki Teiichi (*P.38*) in the early *Showa* period (around 1933), when he created the "Shokado bento" as a light meal to be served during tea ceremony. The divides in the box allow the simultaneous serving of various dishes, regardless of temperature or whether there is broth. It is also a wonderful option for sampling kaiseki ryori at an affordable price.

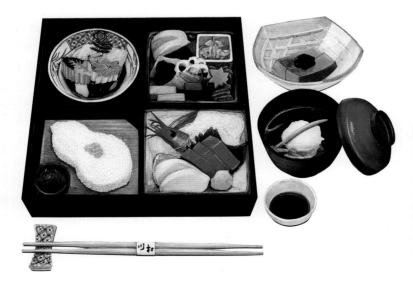

冠婚葬祭などフォーマルな集まりでは、会席料理風に盛込んだ豪華なケータリング弁当「仕出し弁当」が、来客のもてなしによく利用される
Shidashi bento is a type of up-scale catered bento for ceremonial occasions. The kaiseki-style dishes change depending on the type of event.

WASHOKU
Ingredients

食 材

TOFU
& daizu shokuhin
豆腐と大豆食品
tofu and soy products

1. Momentofu
木綿豆腐 *firm tofu*
2. Kinugoshitofu 絹ごし豆腐
silken tofu **3.** Yakitofu 焼き豆腐 *broiled tofu*
4. Atsuage 厚揚げ *thick deep fried tofu* **5.** Oborotofu おぼ
ろ豆腐 *tofu curd* **6.** Usuage 薄揚げ *thin deep fried tofu* **7.**
Ganmodoki がんもどき *deep fried tofu ball* **8.** Tofuyo 豆腐
よう *Okinawan fermented tofu* **9.** Okara おから *soy pulp*
10. Yuba ゆば *tofu skin* **11.** Natto 納豆 *fermented soy bean*

肉食禁止時代を支えた、畑のお肉
The "Meat" of the Field
that Fed Japan During Prohibition

　豆腐の発祥は中国ですが、柔らかくて味が淡
白な日本の豆腐は食材としても応用が広く、肉
食を禁じられていた時代の日本では、庶民のタ
ンパク源として様々な料理で食べられていまし
た。江戸時代には『豆腐百珍』という、100種
類もの豆腐料理を紹介した料理本が刊行されて
います。

　豆腐は、吸水させた大豆をすりつぶして加熱
し、絞った豆乳ににがり（塩化マグネシウム）を
加えて固めてつくります。これを水にさらした
ものが、柔らかな絹ごし豆腐。脱水したものが
木綿豆腐です。焦げ目をつけた焼き豆腐は、濃
い味の料理に向きます。豆腐を揚げたものが油
揚げで、薄揚げと厚揚げがあります。豆腐を崩
して山芋などを加えて丸めて揚げたものが、が
んもどき（*P.106*）です。沖縄の発酵豆腐、豆腐
ようや、豆乳を温めてタンパク質を凝固させた
膜である京都の湯葉など、地方には特色ある大
豆食品もあります。豆乳の絞りかす「おから」
は、食物繊維が豊富でローカロリーなため、ダ
イエット食材として人気です。

Tofu originated in China, but because it is soft and mild, Japanese tofu can be eaten in many different ways. It was thus the beloved source of protein in Japan during the long period of meat prohibition and is still often called "meat" of the field. In fact, a cookbook called *Tofu Hyakuchin* that introduced 100 tofu dishes was published during the Edo period, illustrating the fact that tofu was an integral part of the Japanese diet.

Tofu is made from soy milk, which is made by soaking, grinding, and boiling soy beans in water. The soy milk is then coagulated by adding *nigari*, which is magnesium chloride. Silken tofu is made by setting the coagulated tofu in water, while firm tofu is made by pressing the moisture out. *Yakitofu* is braised tofu which is suited for dishes with bold flavors, and *aburaage* is deep fried tofu, which can be either thick or thin. *Ganmodoki* (*P.106*) is mashed tofu mixed with mountain potato or other vegetables, shaped into spheres and fried. There are various other regional soy products such as *tofuyo*, which is Okinawan fermented tofu, and *yuba*, which is a specialty of Kyoto made from the film of protein that forms on the surface of hot soy milk. *Okara*, or soy pulp, is a byproduct of tofu left over from making soy milk. High in fiber and low in calories, it is popular as a health food.

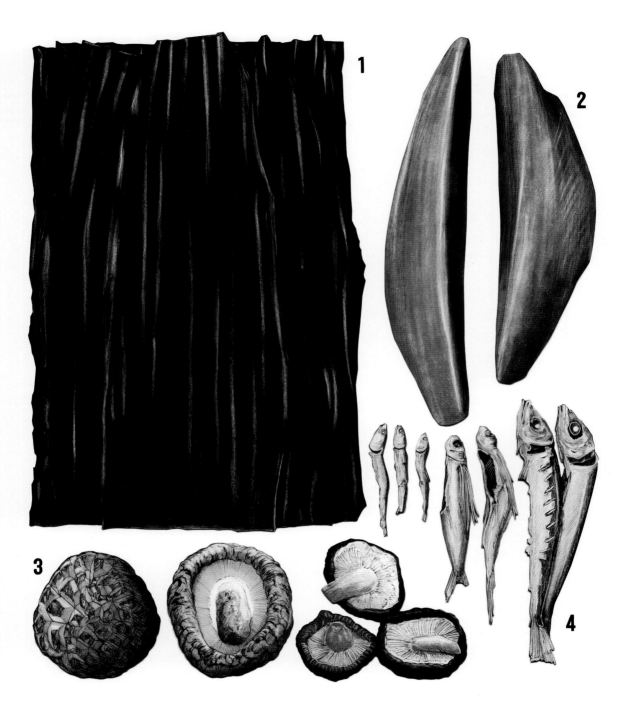

1. Kombu 昆布 *kombu kelp* **2.** Katsuobushi 鰹節 *dried bonito fillet* **3.** Hoshi Shiitake 干しシイタケ *dried shiitake mushrooms* **4.** Niboshi 煮干し *dried sardines*

DASHI sozai
ダシの素材
dashi broth ingredients

Katsuobushi kezuriki 鰹節削り器 *dried bonito fillet shaver*

歳月が育てる うま味の素
Umami Nurtured by Mother Nature and Time

　うま味とは、甘さ、塩辛さ、苦さ、酸っぱさの4つの原味に次ぐ「第五の味」。和食がヘルシーだと言われる理由は、カロリーがほとんどなく栄養素の豊富なダシのうま味をベースにしているからです。ダシの素材には、主に鰹節と昆布。煮干しや干しシイタケも用いられます。うま味成分のグルタミン酸を含む昆布は北海道原産で、生育に2年、収穫してさらに2年熟成させます。知床半島の「羅臼（らうす）」など、収穫地の名前で呼ばれ、産地に格付けがあり、収穫年で出来が評価されるところはワインに似ています。鰹節は、煮たカツオの切り身を煙で燻して乾かし、カビを付けて脂肪と水分を抜いて、タンパク質からうま味成分のイノシン酸を生成させます。約2年かけて出来上がった鰹節は石のような硬さです。

　一般的なダシの引き方は、水に昆布をひたして火にかけ、沸騰寸前で引き上げ、薄く削った鰹節を加えます。長い歳月をかけてつくられた昆布と鰹節からうま味が放出されるのは、あっという間です。

Umami, which translates to savory flavor, is one of the five basic tastes after the other four of sweet, salty, bitter, and sour. One of the reasons Japanese cuisine is deemed healthy is because of dashi, a flavor base that is gentle, low in calories, and full of nutrients. The essential ingredients of dashi broth are bonito flakes and kombu kelp, but dried sardines and shiitake mushrooms are also commonly used. Kombu kelp, which is rich in glutamic acid—one of the chemical components of umami—is mostly from Hokkaido, where it is grown for two years before harvesting, and aged for another two years. Similar to wine, kombu kelp are named by place of harvest, like the "Rausu kombu" from Rausu, Shiretoko Peninsula, for example. They are also rated and evaluated based on production area and harvest year. *Katsuobushi* or bonito flakes on the other hand, are made by smoking and drying simmered bonito fillet. The dried fillets are then cultured with mold: a process that removes fat and moisture and generates inosinic acid, another chemical component of umami. After a two-year process, the fillet is rock-hard and resembles wood.

Although the umami takes years to capture and mature, it is quickly released when making dashi broth.

SAKE
日本酒 *sake*

水、風土、米の磨き方、そして酒器でも変わる繊細な味
Water, Climate, Rice, and Vessel

　日本酒は、原酒ではアルコール度数が世界一高い醸造酒といわれます。ほぼ透明で酸が少なく、香りが地味なため、ワインに比べると個性がないように思われますが、産地、製法、そして飲み方で無限の味わいが広がります。

　日本酒は米を蒸し、麹 (*P.108*) を付けた米と水とを混ぜ、酵母を添加し発酵させてつくります。大別して、米と麹だけを原料としたコクのある純米酒と、アルコールを添加した本醸造酒の２種があります。表面を削り取った米を使うのが、フルーティーな芳香の吟醸酒・大吟醸酒です。醸造は、水や風土から大きく影響を受けるため、産地ごとに特徴があり、近年では発泡日本酒、フルーツ日本酒などユニークな酒造りを試みる蔵元も増えています。

　酒器で味わいがガラリと変わるのも日本酒の楽しみです。やきもの、ガラス、塗り物などでできた「ぐいのみ」は小さな工芸品。コレクションする人も多くいます。温めた酒、燗酒を徳利からぐいのみに注いで飲むのは、日本酒好きの至福のひと時です。

Nihonshu or *sake* is said to have the highest natural alcohol content of all brewed beverages in the world. Because it is a clear beverage with subtle aroma and very little acid, it is often thought to have less character than wine, but in reality sake varies infinitely depending on production area, brewing method, and how it is served.

Sake is made by fermenting a mixture of steamed rice, *koji (P.108)* rice, and water by adding yeast. There are roughly two categories of sake; *junmai* sake, ("junmai" meaning "pure rice") which is made from only sake and koji, and *honjozo* sake, which is fortified with a small amount of alcohol. *Ginjo* sake and *daiginjo* sake are made from rice that has been polished down, and has a fruity aroma. Sake brewing is greatly affected by water quality and the environment, which creates wonderful regional diversity. Today, many sake breweries are experimenting with new sakes such as effervescent sakes and fruit sakes.

Sake vessels are also important, as they can completely change the drinking experience. Made from ceramics, glass, or lacquer, sake cups are small artisanal treasures, and there are many enthusiastic collectors. Drinking hot sake poured from a *tokkuri* (ceramic sake vessel) is a sake lover's moment of bliss.

TSUKEMONO

漬物 *pickles*

白いご飯のパートナー
The Perfect Companion for White Rice

パンにとってのバターと同様、ご飯の相棒が漬物。中でも梅干しは、白い米との紅白のコントラストが日本の国旗「日の丸」になぞらえられる、日本のソウルフードです。漬物は食品の保存方法として、中国をはじめアジア全域で作られていて、日本にも3000種を超える漬物があるといわれます。醤油漬け、麹漬け、酒粕漬けなど、漬け床によって味もさまざま。もっとも親しまれている「ぬか漬け」の漬け床は、乳酸発酵させた米のぬかです。ぬかには精米によって米から失われたビタミンB1が含まれている上、乳酸菌の活動を助ける野菜の食物繊維が一緒にとれるため、シンバイオティクス※健康食としても再評価されています。

　ご飯離れとともに伝統的な漬物の消費が減る中、人気なのが「あっさり漬け」または「浅漬け」。うま味のきいた昆布ダシの調味液で野菜を漬け込んだ、塩分控えめ、新鮮さを味わうサラダ感覚の漬物です。

※腸内環境の改善などに役立つとされる善玉微生物（プロバイオティクスと呼ぶ）と、善玉微生物の餌となって善玉微生物を増やす食品成分（プレバイオティクス）とを、一緒に摂取すること。

Just like butter and bread, *tsukemono* or Japanese pickles and rice are best friends. *Umeboshi* or salted plum in particular, is a classic comfort food with symbolic significance, because the contrast between the red plum against white rice is associated with the Japanese flag. Pickles are made all over Asia as a way to preserve food, and there are over 3,000 different kinds of tsukemono within Japan alone. The flavors vary depending on the pickling base, which are flavored with ingredients like soy sauce, koji, or sake lees. *Nukazuke*, a classic favorite, is a tsukemono that is lacto-fermented in a bed of rice bran. Nukazuke pickles are not only a great source of vitamin B1 from the rice bran, which is shed from white rice in the milling process, but are also gaining recognition as a symbiotic food* because the vegetable fibers help lactobacillus activity in the gut.

Although with the departure from rice, consumption of traditional pickles is declining, lightly pickled tsukemono called "*asazuke*" or "*assari-zuke*" are gaining popularity. Pickled in a low-salt brine rich infused with kelp umami, asazuke are refreshing pickles that can be enjoyed like a salad.

* symbiotic foods combine the characteristics of the probiotics and prebiotics (fiber) which nourish the microorganisms that benefit the host.

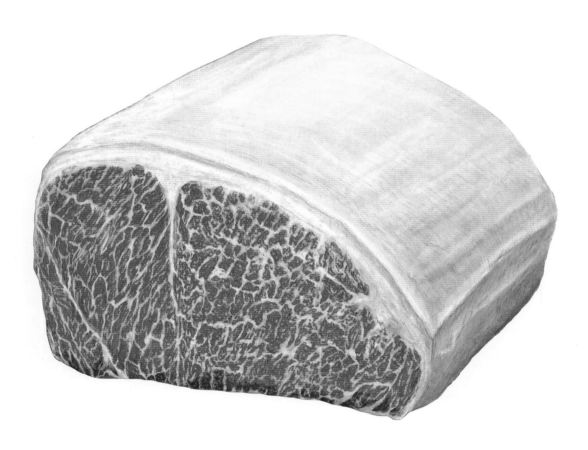

WAGYU

和牛 *Japanese beef*

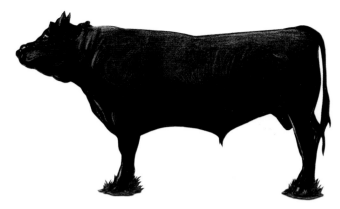

Kuroge Wagyu 黒毛和牛 *Japanese Black*

舌の上でとろける、食の工芸品
Artisanal Meat that Melts on the Tongue

　舌の上でとろける食感が、まるで寿司のトロのような霜降りの和牛。赤身に脂肪が網目のように入っている状態は、大理石の模様になぞらえてマーブリングと呼ばれます。日本の牛肉にはA5を最高とする格付けがあり、一頭からとれる枝肉の割合、肉の色ツヤとキメの細かさ、そしてこのマーブリングの美しさが評価の基準になります。明治4年（1871）に肉食が解禁されてから日本での牛肉づくりは始まりましたが、西欧に比べて後発である上、輸入肉との競争にもさらされました。そのため、農家では独自の食味を求め、ビールを飲ませてマッサージする、畳の上で育てる、クラシック音楽を聴かせるなど、まるで工芸品を磨き上げるような肥育方法も試みられ、1960年代頃には松阪牛、近江牛、神戸牛といった世界的なブランド牛が育ちました。近年では米国やオーストラリア産のWAGYUも流通し、和牛は高級牛肉の代名詞となっています。

Rich, beautifully marbled *wagyu* meat melts on the tongue, almost like *toro* fatty tuna sushi. In Japanese, the marbling of the meat is called "*shimo-furi*," a term that refers to the white spots in the meat that look like a frosted field. Japanese beef has a grading system of which "A5" is the highest; it is based on the amount of quality meat one cow can yield, the color, shine, and smoothness of the meat, and the aesthetic beauty of the marbling. Beef production in Japan started when the meat ban was lifted in the 4th year of the Meiji period (1871). Japanese beef farmers faced the challenge of learning the trade from scratch, as well as competing with imported meat. In pursuit of quality, they tried elaborate methods like giving the cattle beer and massages, raising them on *tatami* mats, and playing classical music. This craftsmanship gave way to premium brands such as Matsuzaka beef, Omi beef, and Kobe beef. Today, Japanese beef produced in the U.S. and Australia are popular as well, and wagyu is recognized across the globe as a synonym for premium beef.

NIHONCHA

日本茶 *Japanese tea*

昔・苦い一服、いま・甘いスイーツになった抹茶
Once Avoided for its Bitterness, Matcha Gains Popularity

　日本のお茶の代名詞、緑茶の原料は、紅茶やウーロン茶と同じ茶の木の葉です。葉を摘んだ後に発酵させず、葉を蒸して揉んで乾燥させてつくらることから、独特のほろ苦さと爽やかさがあります。煎じて（抽出して）飲む緑茶を煎茶と言い、これに炒った玄米を加えたものが玄米茶。ほうじ茶は茶葉を焙煎したものです。高級茶として知られる玉露は、茶の木に覆いをかけて日陰で育て、甘みと旨みを凝縮させた葉を煎茶と同様の製法でつくります。抹茶は玉露と同様、日光を遮って育てた葉を使い、揉まずに乾燥させて石臼で挽き、粉末にした茶をお湯で溶いて茶筅で撹拌します。葉を丸ごと飲むという、世界的にも珍しいお茶です。この抹茶を儀式的な作法で飲むのが、日本を代表する芸道「茶の湯」です。長らく、そんな茶の湯の堅苦しいイメージもあってか、抹茶といえば「苦い」と敬遠する人が多かったのですが、コーヒーチェーンの抹茶シェイクと、抹茶味のスイーツの登場で、抹茶人気は世界に広がりました。健康食としての注目度も高まっています。

　Green tea, which is synonymous with Japanese tea, is made from the same tea leaves used to make black tea or *oolong* tea. The difference is that the harvested leaves are not fermented. Instead, they are steamed, kneaded, and dried, which results in a particular bitter and fresh flavor. Everyday steeped green tea is called *sencha*; *genmaicha* is a variation with roasted brown rice, and *hojicha* is roasted tea leaves. *Gyokuro* is a high grade tea that is also steeped. It is made with the same process as sencha, but the tea leaves are grown in the shade in order to bring out sweetness and umami. *Matcha* is also made from tea leaves grown in the shade, but the tea leaves are dried without kneading. The dried leaves are then ground with a stone mill into a fine powder, which is mixed with hot water with a bamboo whisk called *chasen*. The fact that the tea leaves are mixed in and consumed with the water makes matcha a rather unusual tea. *Chanoyu* or Tea Ceremony is the practice of drinking this tea in a ceremonial manner. For a long time, many considered matcha unpleasantly bitter and uptight because of the rigidity associated with Tea Ceremony. However, thanks in part to the rise in matcha flavored desserts and sweeter beverages created by coffee chains, today it has gained popularity across the globe.

SHUN CALENDAR
旬の食材と料理
seasonal Japanese dishes and ingredients

　和食で最も大切なのは季節感。日本人が春夏秋冬、その時とれた旬の食材にこだわるのは、それを食べることで、自然や季節とのつながりを体感しようとするからです。

Above all, Japanese cuisine values seasonal foods. Experiencing the seasons through eating ingredients and dishes specific to the time of the year —called "shun"— is the essence and joy of Japanese cuisine.

Natsuyasai
夏野菜
summer vegetables

Ingen mame インゲン豆 *green beans* / Goya ゴーヤ *bitter melon* / Nasu 茄子 *eggplant* / Uri 瓜 *gourd* / Tomato トマト *tomato* / Shishitou シシトウ *shishito pepper* / Sunappu Endo スナップエンドウ *snap peas* / Toumorokoshi トウモロコシ *corn* / Kyuri きゅうり *cucumber*

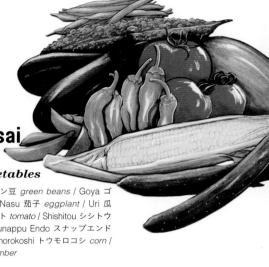

Hamo
鱧 *pike conger*

Hamo Otoshi 鱧落とし *boiled pike conger with salted plum paste*

Somen
そうめん
somen noodles (P.46)

Sansai
山菜 *mountain vegetables*

Sansai Tempura 山菜天ぷら *assorted mountain vegetable tempura (P.24)*

6

春 *Spring*

Takenoko
タケノコ
bamboo shoot

Wakatake Ni 若竹煮 *simmered bamboo shoot and wakame seaweed*

Katsuo
鰹 *skipjack tuna*

Katsuo no Tataki 鰹のタタキ *lightly seared skipjack tuna*

3

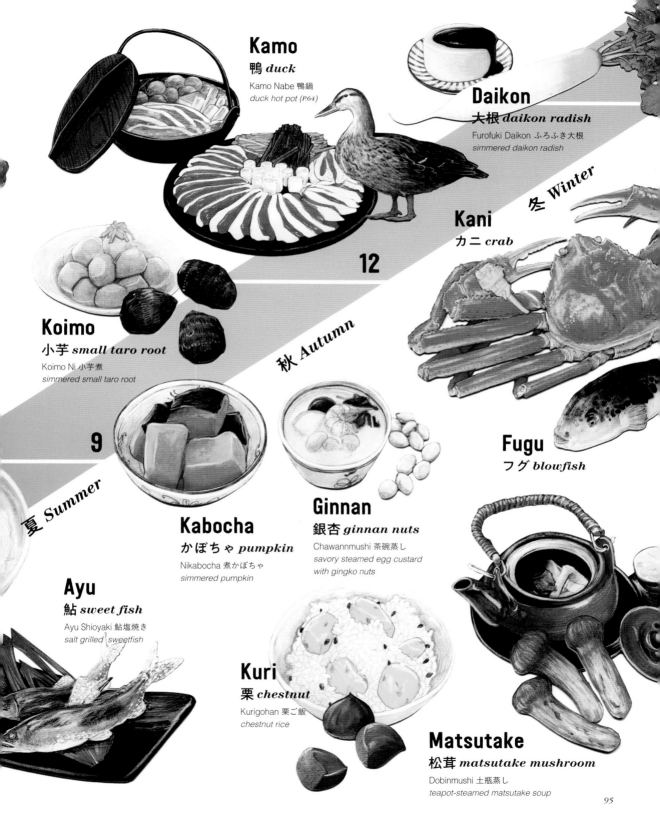

Kamo
鴨 *duck*

Kamo Nabe 鴨鍋
duck hot pot (P.64)

Daikon
大根 *daikon radish*

Furofuki Daikon ふろふき大根
simmered daikon radish

冬 *Winter*

Kani
カニ *crab*

12

Koimo
小芋 *small taro root*

Koimo Ni 小芋煮
simmered small taro root

秋 *Autumn*

9

夏 *Summer*

Fugu
フグ *blowfish*

Kabocha
かぼちゃ *pumpkin*

Nikabocha 煮かぼちゃ
simmered pumpkin

Ginnan
銀杏 *ginnan nuts*

Chawannmushi 茶碗蒸し
*savory steamed egg custard
with gingko nuts*

Ayu
鮎 *sweet fish*

Ayu Shioyaki 鮎塩焼き
salt grilled sweetfish

Kuri
栗 *chestnut*

Kurigohan 栗ご飯
chestnut rice

Matsutake
松茸 *matsutake mushroom*

Dobinmushi 土瓶蒸し
teapot-steamed matsutake soup

寿司職人の華麗なる技、葉蘭
The Haran Beautifully Displays a Sushi Chef's Skill

寿司やお弁当に入っている緑色のプラスチックのシート(P.74)。これを葉蘭(ハラン)と呼びます。もともとは寿司職人が葉蘭という植物の葉や笹の葉を、包丁で様々な形に切って細工して寿司に添えたものでした。葉蘭には揮発性の殺菌物質フィトンチッドが含まれていて防腐の役目をはたし、葉の青さは寿司の鮮度を証明しました。今では本物の葉蘭切り、笹切りを見ることは少なくなりましたが、寿司職人の間では、伝統の技を競うコンクールも続けられています。

The green plastic sheets often seen in sushi takeout or store bought bentos (P.74) are called *haran*. Today, they serve as decorative dividers, but originally, they were made from the leaves of windowsill orchids ("haran") or bamboo that sushi chefs cut into various shapes and placed in sushi takeaways. The orchid and bamboo leaves act as an antiseptic because they contain a volatile anti-microbial substance called phytoncide, and the greenness of the leaves were also a way to prove the freshness of the sushi. Sadly today we do not see the true haran as often, but there are still contests for sushi chefs to compete with their haran-cutting skills.

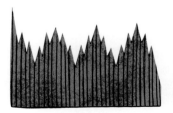

江戸(東京)の握り寿司には、幅の広い隈笹の葉の笹切りが使われる。プラスチックの葉蘭は「バラン」と呼ばれる
Edo-style (classic Tokyo-style) nigiri sushi often uses sasa veitchii, a type of bamboo with wide leaves. Plastic haran are also called "baran".

Washoku Explained

和 食 の 話

KOME 米 *rice*

Gohan ご飯 *rice*

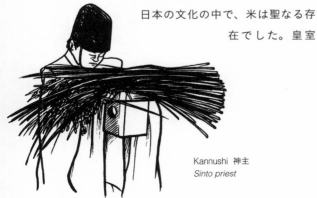

祈りと政治と関わってきた、日本の主食・米

　豪華な会席料理 (*P.38*) のコースの終わりに、白いご飯が出てくることを不思議に思う人は少なくありません。しかも、そのご飯をわざわざ手間をかけて、昔ながらの土鍋で炊く料理人もいます。世界一生産量が多い米は、茹でて食べる細長いインディカ種ですが、日本の米は楕円形のジャポニカ種。甘さと粘りが特色で、水加減、火加減に経験と技術を要する「炊き干し法」で炊きあげます。

Onigiri おにぎり *rice ball*

　食料自給率が3割に満たない日本で米は唯一、ほぼ自給できている農産物です。ご飯は食事と同義語で、食事はラーメンでもカレーでも、すべて「ご飯」と呼ばれます。ご飯は主食であるということ以上に、特別な意味を持っています。日本の文化の中で、米は聖なる存在でした。皇室

Kannushi 神主
Sinto priest

でもっとも重要な祭祀は、稲を刈り取る儀式・新嘗祭 (にいなめさい) です。相撲の起源は米の豊作を祈る儀式でした。米からつくられる酒 (*P.86*) と餅は、神様への捧げもの。神式の結婚式で、新郎新婦は杯 (*P.86*) で酒を飲み交わして夫婦の絆を結び、新年には餅を供えます。米の神聖さは、日本で1200年近く続いた肉食の禁止と関わりがあります。古代社会では、葬いや重要な願い事がある時に動物の肉断ちをして祈る風習がありました。稲作の失敗から免れるため、天武4年 (675) から、肉食が禁じられたのです。それに伴って、米の神聖なイメージは強められました。また、米は世俗的な力も象徴しました。武士が国を治めていた封建時代、米は税として徴収され、大名の収入は石高 (こくだか)、つまり米の収穫量で示されました。

　近代化と安定を得た現在の日本で、米への強い思いは、おいしいご飯の追求へと向けられています。全国でブランド米がつくられ、中でも、新潟・魚沼のコシヒカリは人気の銘柄。電器店では、炊き上がりの食感を微調整するような機能を備えた、ハイスペック炊飯器が、高価にも関わらずよく売れています。歴史と信仰に裏付けられた米へのこだわりが生む日本のご飯のおいしさは、同じ米食の東アジアからの旅行者をも圧倒します。

Rice, Politics, and Sacred Ritual

Some people might wonder why something as simple as white rice is served at the end of a luxurious kaiseki (P.38) course meal. Yet rice is the foundation of Japanese cuisine, and many chefs take the time and effort to cook rice in traditional clay pots. In contrast to the long, thin grains of indica rice, which is the most widely consumed rice in the world, japonica rice is a

Japonika mai
ジャポニカ米
japonica rice

Jabanika mai
ジャバニカ米
javanica rice

Indika mai
インディカ米
indica rice

short-grain rice with a distinct sweetness and viscosity. The water-rice ratio and temperature must be fine-tuned when cooking japonica rice using what is called the absorption method, where it is boiled, simmered over low heat, and steamed.

The word "*gohan*," which means rice in Japanese, also means "meal." A meal is always called "gohan," whether it is ramen or curry on the menu. Although food self-sufficiency is less than 30% in Japan, rice is the one agricultural product that is produced almost entirely domestically. In addition to being the country's staple food, rice is also revered for its cultural significance.

Historically, rice has been regarded as sacred, and is still the focus of many rituals today in Japanese culture. For example, *Niiname-sai*, a ritual of rice harvest, is the most important ritual held in the Imperial Household of Japan. Sumo wrestling is a sport that actually evolved from a ritual of praying for good rice harvest. In *Shinto*, Japan's indigenous religion, sake (P.86) or rice wine and mochi rice cake are important

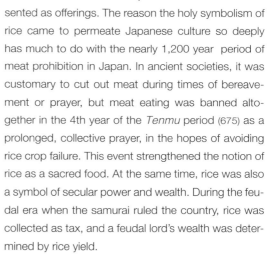

Donabe 土鍋
clay pot

traditional offerings. In Shinto weddings, the bride and groom drink sake from a lacquer sake cup (P.86) together in a ritual of bonding, and during the New Year, rice cakes are presented as offerings. The reason the holy symbolism of rice came to permeate Japanese culture so deeply has much to do with the nearly 1,200 year period of meat prohibition in Japan. In ancient societies, it was customary to cut out meat during times of bereavement or prayer, but meat eating was banned altogether in the 4th year of the *Tenmu* period (675) as a prolonged, collective prayer, in the hopes of avoiding rice crop failure. This event strengthened the notion of rice as a sacred food. At the same time, rice was also a symbol of secular power and wealth. During the feudal era when the samurai ruled the country, rice was collected as tax, and a feudal lord's wealth was determined by rice yield.

In today's modernized, stabilized Japan however, this passion and respect for rice has shifted to the pursuit of delicious rice. Premium brands of rice are produced nationwide, of which Koshihikari, made in Uonuma, Niigata prefecture, is particularly popular. High-performance rice cookers that allow for the fine-tuning of texture are also popular items sold at electronics stores. This extraordinary commitment to rice is backed by historic and religious significance, and perhaps the reason Japanese rice can sometimes surprise visitors from other rice-eating countries in East Asia.

Inaho 稲穂
ear of rice

HOCHO 包丁 *knife*

サムライの魂は刀、料理人の命は包丁

　和食の料理人に求められる最も重要な技は、切ることです。和食で一番のごちそうである刺身(*P.22*)は、どう切るかによって、味が大きく左右されます。料理人は「包丁人」とも呼ばれ、一人前になるまでには、長い年月の包丁修業が求められます。和食では西洋料理と違って、皿の上でナイフを使いません。料理人は食材を箸でつまんで食べやすくしておくことはもちろん、歯ごたえや食べ心地をよくするために、料理ごとに決められた食材の切り方を知っておかねばなりません。このほか「剥きもの」と呼ばれる花や紅葉の形の飾り切り、大根を紙のように薄く剥く「かつら剥き」など、料理の見た目を彩る工芸的な細工もあれば、煮物の味が染みやすくするための隠し包丁、煮崩れを防ぐ面取りなど、おいしさを影で支える包丁仕事もあります。

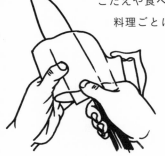

Katsuramuki かつら剥き
paper thin daikon sheets

　料理人は、こうした用途や素材に合わせて、数多くの中から包丁を選びます。魚を切る出刃包丁、刺身を引く刺身(柳刃)包丁、野菜を切る菜切り包丁、細工用のペティナイフ。ほかに鱧(*P.94*)、蛸、寿司(*P.14*)、鰻(*P.26*)、麺類、西瓜や栗にも、それ

ぞれ専用の包丁があります。

　日本の包丁は、江戸時代に侍の刀をつくっていた刀鍛冶がつくりはじめました。刺身包丁は日本刀と同じ片刃で、魚の細胞を壊さずにはがすように切れるので、引き切った刺身の角がシャープに立ち、断面は舌触り良くなめらかになるのです。刺身を引く(切る)時には、料理人は手先に伝わる食材の感触を確かめながら包丁を使います。西洋の包丁が頑丈さを、中国の包丁が重さを重視するのに比べて、日本の包丁はあたかも手先の延長であるかのように、しなやかさに動くことを重視します。サムライの魂は刀、料理人の命は包丁。鋭い切れ味を保つため、料理人は毎日、砥石での手入れを欠かしません。

Deba bocho 出刃包丁 *meat knife* / Nakiri bocho 菜切包丁 *vegetable knife* / Sushikiri bocho 寿司切り包丁 *rolled sushi knife* / Takobiki bocho 蛸挽き包丁 *octopus knife* / Yanagiba bocho 柳刃包丁 *sashimi knife*

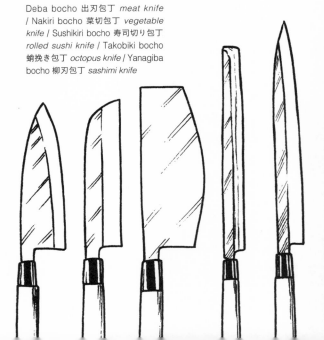

Mukimono 剥きもの
decorative garnishing

A Sword is a Samurai's Soul; A Knife is a Chef's Life

Cutting skills are arguably a chef's most important skill in Japanese cuisine. Sashimi (*P.22*), which is one of the most revered dishes in Japanese cuisine, is a great example of a dish that largely depends on cutting technique. A chef —also called a *hocho-nin* ("knife master")— must train for many years to acquire the required knife skills. Because knives are not used on the plate in Japanese cuisine, a chef must be mindful to cut the ingredients into sizes and shapes that are easy to lift with chopsticks. There are also rules for each dish about which cutting method is appropriate to optimize the texture and mouthfeel of each ingredient. It is also important to learn the delicate skill of making ornamental elements, such as ingredients cut into the shapes of flowers or leaves (*mukimono*), and *katsuramuki* or daikon radish peeled into paper thin sheets. Some important knife work is invisible, like *kakushibocho*, which are incisions that help ingredients soak up the dashi flavors, and *mentori*, a process of removing corners in order to keep simmered foods from falling apart. These various knife skills support the very foundation of Japanese cuisine.

A chef will always consider both the particular qualities of an ingredient and its cooking method before choosing the appropriate knife. The foundational knives include *deba bocho* (a thick knife for fish and meat), *yanagiba bocho* (a long narrow knife for cutting sashimi), *nakiri bocho* (a thin knife for chopping vegetables), and

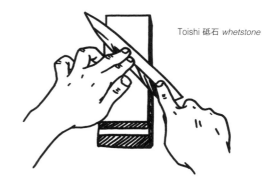

Toishi 砥石 *whetstone*

petty knife for decorative work. There are also knives specifically designed for single ingredients like pike conger (*p.94*), octopus, rolled sushi (*p.14*), eel (*p.26*), noodles, watermelon and chestnuts.

Japanese culinary knives as we know them today were crafted by samurai sword-smiths during the Edo period. The blade of a sashimi knife, like the blade of a Japanese sword, is one sided, and can separate fish cells without breaking them, which creates a deliciously smooth surface. It's often said that "a sword is a samurai's soul, and a knife is a chef's life." Chefs must use a whetstone everyday to keep their knives sharp.

Samurai & Katana 侍と刀
samurai & sword

topic 3
HASHI 箸 *chopsticks*

箸は、あなたの一部分

迷い箸、涙箸、振り上げ箸‥‥。これらは全て、マナー違反の箸づかい。食べ物の上で箸をウロウロと動かしたり、箸から汁を垂らしたり、箸で人や物を指すなど、和食のテーブルマナーで、やってはいけないことが、箸の使い方の中には数多くあります。なぜ日本人がこんなに箸づかいに神経質なのか？　それは、箸がその人の身体の延長であるかのように感じられるからかもしれません。

箸は、中国、朝鮮半島、ベトナムなどで使われていますが、日本の箸の特徴は、個人専用の「属人器」であること。つまり、箸はそれぞれの人専用で、家族であっても共用しません。そのように、箸はきわめて私的なカトラリーなので、食堂などでは、不特定多数の人と同じ箸を使うより、使い捨ての箸が好まれます。一度、自分の箸が触れた料理を他の人にすすめることや、皆で食べる大皿の料理を自分の箸で取ることはタブーです。箸で料理を取り分ける時は、誰のものでもない中間的な「取り箸」が使われます。

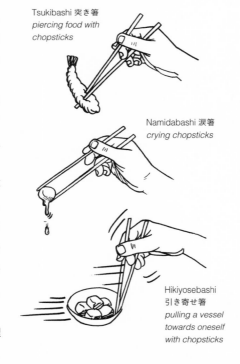

Tsukibashi 突き箸
piercing food with chopsticks

Namidabashi 涙箸
crying chopsticks

Hikiyosebashi 引き寄せ箸
pulling a vessel towards oneself with chopsticks

自分以外の誰かと共用する唯一の箸が、お正月におせち料理 (P.41) を食べる「祝い箸」です。これは、両方の端がものをつまむ箸先として削られているので、「両口箸」とも呼ばれます。ふたつの箸先は、人と神様とが共に食事をすることを意味しているのです。

箸は多機能なカトラリーで、ご飯をまとめて口に運んだり、麺類をすすったり、魚の身を骨から外したり、味噌汁などの汁物も箸を使って食べます。汁椀を持ち上げて口をつけて飲むことは、箸を使うことから生まれた和食の作法です。

箸先が細く削られている日本の箸は、細かな作業にも向いているため、食卓だけでなく、調理場でも、「はさむ」「まぜる」「盛り付け」のための、万能調理器具として活躍します。厨房の料理人のトップは、先端が通常よりも細い「花板箸」を持って、料理の盛り付けを細やかに仕上げます。

Hashioki 箸置き *chopstick rest*

Chopsticks as an Extension of the Self

Hovering over food with chopsticks ("wandering chopsticks"), dripping liquid while holding food with chopsticks ("crying chopsticks"), and pointing at things or people with chopsticks ("raised chopsticks") are some of the major taboos in Japanese chopsticks etiquette. The reason Japanese people are so particular about their chopsticks may be because they can feel like an extensions of the self.

Chopsticks are used in China, the Korean peninsula, and Vietnam among other countries, but one unique aspect of Japanese chopsticks is how they are considered personal utensils. At

Iwaibashi 祝い箸 *celebration chopsticks*

home, each individual has their own pair which is not shared even among family members. Because it is a personal item, people often prefer disposable chopsticks over reusable communal chopsticks at cafeterias and food courts. One must also be mindful of where one's chopsticks go; Using personal chopsticks to offer food or take food from a communal dish is also taboo. Instead, designated serving chopsticks are used for serving communal dishes.

The one time chopsticks are shared is on New Year's Day, when special celebration chopsticks called iwaibashi are used to eat osechi ryori (*P.41*). They are also referred to as "double-ended chopsticks" because they are carved to a narrow point on both ends instead of just one end. The top end is reserved for the *Toshigami* ("Year God") deity and thus represents the sharing of food with a god.

Chopsticks are versatile utensils that can hold rice, hoist noodles, and pick fish meat off the bone. One etiquette rule unique to Japanese cuisine is the way soups are picked up from the table and sipped directly from the edge of the bowl. This is because soups are also eaten with chopsticks. Japanese chopsticks are carved to a point, which makes them suitable for precision. This is part of the reason chopsticks also shine in the kitchen as an all-purpose utensil, for everything from grabbing and mixing to plating. Some chefs use what is called a *hanaitabashi* ("hanaita" meaning top chef) a very thin, delicate pair of chopsticks for precise plating.

Toribashi 取り箸
*chopsticks for serving
a communal dish*

UTSUWA 器 *vessels*

「器は料理の着物」。味わう前に眼で食べる

陶芸家で美食家の北大路魯山人(1883-1959)は「器は料理の着物」と言いました。高級な割烹や会席料理(P.38)の店に行くと、コース料理が様々な器とともに登場し、まるで器のファッションショーのようです。器と料理の盛り付けの美しい調和が「眼で食べる」といわれる和食の鑑賞ポイントです。

着物と同様、器にもっとも大切なのは季節感で、日本料理店では春夏秋冬で器の「衣替え」をします。春は漆器のお椀に桜の蒔絵、夏のお刺身はガラスの鉢に、秋は紅葉の形のお皿に八寸を。冬は暖かな土味の陶器が焼き物に映えます。季節にふさわしい器の「着こなし」ができるよう、膨大な数の器とそのための倉庫を持っている料理人も珍しくありません。

和食の器の中でとくにバリエーションが豊富なのは、やきものです。やきものには、白く薄くなめらかな手触りの磁器と、「土もの」と呼ばれる陶器があります。陶器には釉薬で覆われているものと、土の風合いを生かした焼締(やきし

Oribe Orikomizara
織部折込鉢
Oribe folded plate

め)があります。陶器の器は吸水性があるため、ソースを大切にする西洋料理ではあまり使われません。

これも着物と同様で、和食の器には、古典もあればモードもあります。老舗料理店は、代々受け継がれてきた骨董の器でおもてなしに風格を添えます。もし出て来た古い器にキズを修繕した跡、金継ぎがあったら、それは直してでもお客様にお出ししたい貴重な器の証です。逆に、若い料理人が斬新な現代陶芸作家の器で、新鮮なプレゼンテーションを試みることもあります。クラフトの盛んな日本には、料理のための器を作る陶芸家が数多く活躍しています。料理人にとって器は単なる容れ物ではなく、アイデンティティの表現であり、また、料理にインスピレーションを与えてくれるものでもあります。和食をいただく時は、料理と一体になった器の魅力も味わってください。

Kosometsuke 古染付 *blue and white porcelain mukozuke plate from Ming dynasty China*

Senmengata Mukoduke
扇面型向付 *folding fan-shaped mukozuke plate*

Manaitazara 俎皿
"cutting board" plate

Vessels as a "Kimono" for food: the Art of Eating with Your Eyes Before Tasting

Ceramicist and gastronomer Kitaoji Rosanjin (1883-1959) said that "tableware is the *kimono* of food." In upscale Japanese cuisine and kaiseki (*P.38*) restaurant, the courses arrive in various beautiful vessels, almost as if it were a fashion show of plates and bowls. Japanese food is often described as a cuisine to "eat with

Rinkabachi 輪花鉢
flower shaped bowl

the eyes," particularly in the way the vessels harmonize beautifully with the food and plating. Like kimonos, it is important that vessels express the season. A *maki-e* lacquer bowl adorned with golden cherry blossoms for the spring, and glass bowls for the summer; perhaps a leaf-shaped plate for the autumn hassun appetizer, and a warm, earthy ceramic plate for winter *yakimono* (grilled dish). Many chefs have an extensive vessel collection as well as a designated storage space so they can "dress" their food appropriately.

The category among Japanese vessels with the most variety is pottery, of which there are two types: white, thin, and smooth porcelain ware, and thick, earthy ceramic ware. Ceramic vessels are either finished with glaze or fired without; the latter, called *yakishime*, emphasizes the natural texture

Meshiwan 飯碗
rice bowl

and color of the clay. Because ceramic vessels tend to absorb moisture, they are seldom used in Western cuisine where sauce is often an important element.

Much like kimono, Japanese vessels can vary a great deal in style as well between classical and contemporary. Long-established restaurants take pride in stately presentations using antique vessels passed down through the generations. If a presented vessel appears to have been mended with gold, that means it is a vessel valuable enough to use in spite of the defect. It is a sign of respect towards customers. Contrastingly, there are also many young chefs experimenting with their presentations using stylish vessels by contemporary ceramicists. Handicrafts are a vital part of Japanese culture, and many potters are prolific vessel-makers. To a chef, a vessel is not just a vehicle for food, but also an expression of identity, and a source of inspiration and creativity. Admiring the vessel in unison with the food is the key to fully enjoy the experience of Japanese cuisine.

Kakuzara 角皿
square plate

Warizansho 割山椒
"cracked Japanese pepper" bowl

SHOJIN RYORI 精進料理
Japanese Zen Buddhist cuisine

和食の悟りもひらいた精進料理

　禅は、精神を変革するプラクティスとして世界で注目されていますが、和食にも大きな変革を起こしました。禅が日本にもたらされたのは13世紀。中国の宋で禅を学んだ道元（1200-1253）は曹洞宗の開祖となり、精進料理を日本に伝えました。道元は「料理すること、食べることも、禅の大切な修行である」と説いて、日本で初めて食べることについて哲学的に考察しました。

　僧院では、禅僧自らが食事を作ります。料理担当の僧は、「典座（てんぞ）」と呼ばれ、生き物を殺すことを禁じる戒律を守りながら、植物性の素材だけで美味しい料理を工夫します。「精進」という言葉には、修行にあたって一心に努力や工夫をするという意味もあるのです。この精進から、多くの和食の料理法が発展しました。干瓢（かんぴょう）（P.17）などからとったダシのうま味で野菜を味付ける煮物（P.78）、すり鉢を使って味噌やゴマ、くるみ、豆類や豆腐など複数の味覚を調合する和え物（P.76）、油で揚げてボリュームを出す揚げ物（P.24）。

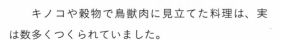

Zensou & Suribachi　禅僧とすり鉢
Zen monk with a mortar

これが一般にも知れ渡り、それ以前にはゆでるか焼くしかなかった料理を大きく変えてゆき、和食は豊かになってゆきました。観光地のお寺の近くにある精進料理店では、肉なしでも満足できるよう僧たちが工夫した胡麻豆腐や高野豆腐などの料理を、洗練させたかたちで食べさせてくれます。

　日本の精進料理の中でユニークなのが、江戸時代に伝わった中国式の禅宗・黄檗宗の精進料理「普茶料理（ふちゃ）」で、肉や魚そっくりの「もどき料理」に特徴があります。一般に、日本の精進料理には、肉をもどく料理は鳥のガンの肉に似せた「がんもどき」（P.82）くらいしかないように思われていることから、中国式精進の「もどき料理」に抵抗を感じる日本人は少なくありません。しかし、もともと精進料理は肉に近い味わいや食感をもとめることから発展したもので、表向き肉食が禁じられた時代の日本の僧院の中でも、キノコや穀物で鳥獣肉に見立てた料理は、実は数多くつくられていました。

How Zen Buddhism Enlightened Japanese Cooking

Zen Buddhism is gaining attention globally as a practice that transforms the spirit, but it is also something that has profoundly transformed Japanese cuisine. Zen Buddhism was brought to Japan during the 13th century by the Buddhist priest Dogen (1200-1253), who studied Zen in Song dynasty China. Dogen is accredited for establishing the *Soto* school of Zen in Japan, but he is also known for having brought back shojin ryori (Buddhist cuisine). Dogen preached that "cooking and eating are important Zen practices;" this was one of the earliest philosophical observations on the act of eating recorded in Japanese history.

Shojinryori 精進料理 *shojin ryori set meal*

In a Zen monastery, the monks themselves are responsible for preparing meals. Called "*tenzo*," the monks in charge of the cooking abide by the rules that prohibit the taking of animal lives, and devise creative ways to cook delicious, sustaining meals with plant-based ingredients. The word "shojin" also means to fully dedicate oneself to training, which emphasizes the importance of cooking as part of it. Many dishes in Japanese cuisine such as nimono (simmered foods, see *P.78*), aemono (marinated dishes, see *P.76*) which are prepared in a mortar, and fried foods (*P.24*) are prepared with the cooking methods that evolved from shojin ryori. In other words, Japanese cooking, which was previously limited to simpler methods like grilling and boiling, was transformed by the innovations within shojin ryori. Deep frying was introduced as a way to enhance satisfaction, and complex processes like simmering vegetables in umami-rich dried gourd (*P.17*) broth, or mixing vegetables with miso, sesame seeds, walnuts, or soy beans, were devised to combine and deepen flavors. Buddhist cuisine restaurants near Zen temples are open to tourists and a great way to experience a refined Buddhist meal with sustaining vegetarian items like *koyadofu* (dehydrated tofu) or *gomadofu* (sesame tofu).

One particular style of Buddhist cuisine characterized by dishes that feature mock meat is the Chinese-style Buddhist cuisine *fucha ryori* from the *Obaku-shu* school of Zen, which was brought to Japan during the Edo period. Because not many Japanese Buddhist mock meat foods are prevalent in the mainstream aside from ganmodoki (deep fried tofu balls that resemble goose meat, see *P.82*), some Japanese people feel resistant towards them. However, it is important to note that Buddhist cuisine evolved out of the desire to create textures and flavors similar to meat; there is a long history of using mushrooms, grains, and beans to mimic meat, even in Japan, where meat had been banned for so long.

topic 6
MISO & SHOYU 味噌と醤油
miso and soy sauce

Takujo Shoyu 卓上醤油
table soy sauce

日本の"国菌"麹が醸す、うま味万能調味料

西洋料理では料理ごとにソースを作りますが、和食では、ほとんどの料理の調味に醤油や味噌、酒とみりんが活躍します。これらは全て、麹を使った発酵食品です。麹は酒造りのほか、多くの発酵食づくりに関わる微生物で、日本の「国菌」と呼ばれています。発酵食は、食べ物を保存する知恵として世界の各地でつくられていますが、近代以前の日本では、表向き肉食は禁止されていたので、動物の肉からコクや食べごたえを得ることができず、油脂や砂糖も乏しかったため、発酵から得られるうま味は料理に欠かせないものでした。

醤油の元祖は、奈良時代に中国から伝わった大豆の発酵調味料「醤（ひしほ）」です。薄切りにした魚介などの膾（なます）を、これにつけて食べました。「刺身に醤油」という組み合わせのルーツです。醤油には濃口、薄口があり、関東では濃口、関西では薄口が好まれます。薄口醤油は塩分が多く透明感があり風味が控えめなので、素材の色や香りを生かしたい料理に向いています。

酒とみりんは、煮物を煮る時に加えることで、素材にうま味や甘さを加えます。みりんは日本独自の醸造調味料で、煮物や焼き物のタレに繊細な甘みとおいしそうな照りを出してくれます。

味噌は、蒸した大豆に麹と塩分を加えて発酵・熟成させて作ります。麹の原料によって米味噌、麦味噌、豆味噌があり、まろやかな白味噌から辛めの赤味噌まで、色も味も様々。かつては家庭で仕込んだものでしたが、今は全国各地の醸造所で1000種類以上もの味噌がつくられています。溶いて味噌汁に、焼き物のペーストに、和え衣（P.76）に、そして和菓子にも使われる、まさに万能調味料です。近年、発酵食のヘルシーさが注目されていることから、麹が家庭の台所で再び活躍し始めています。麹を塩で熟成させる「塩麹」は簡単に作ることができて、肉、野菜を漬け込むだけでおいしくなるので、和洋問わない料理に活用されています。

Shoyugura 醤油蔵 *soy sauce brewery*

The Almighty Umami-rich Seasonings Created by Japan's "National Fungus"

Many Western dishes have their own sauces, but in Japanese cuisine, most dishes are seasoned with soy sauce, miso, sake, and mirin, which are all fermented foods made with koji which is also known as the "national mold." Fermented foods are made all over the world as a way to preserve food, but they have been a particularly important part of the Japanese diet because meat eating was prohibited for a long time, and because oils and sugars were rare commodities.

Murasaki むらさき
high quality soy sauce

Soy sauce evolved from a fermented condiment made from soy beans called "*hishio*," which was brought over from China during the Nara period (710-794). It was often eaten with thinly cut marinated seafood, a combination that later evolved into sashimi and soy sauce. There are mainly two types of soy sauce; *usukuchi* soy sauce, which is lighter in color but higher in salt content, and *koikuchi* soy sauce, which is darker in color. Koikuchi is more prevalent in eastern Japan, and usukuchi in Western Japan. Usukuchi soy sauce is subtle in both color and aroma, which makes it more suitable for dishes that emphasize the original colors and flavors of the ingredients.

Akamiso & Shiromiso
赤味噌と白味噌
red & white miso

Sake and mirin are added to simmered dishes to give the ingredients a pleasant umami and sweetness. Mirin is a fermented seasoning unique to Japan with a delicate sweetness that has a beautiful glazing effect on simmered or grilled dishes.

Miso Shiru 味噌汁
miso soup

Miso is made by fermenting and aging steamed soybeans with koji and salt. There are varieties such as rice miso, barley miso, and bean miso, depending on the type of koji, and the colors can vary from a mild white miso to a more robust red miso, depending on the fermentation process. Miso was once something that was made in the home, but today, there are over 1,000 different kinds of miso made in breweries nationwide. It is truly an almighty condiment that can be made into miso soup, used as a marinade for grilled dishes, added to dressings (*P.76*), and even used in traditional Japanese sweets. With fermented foods on the rise in recent years, *shio-koji* or rice koji aged with salt is gaining popularity. It is not only easy to make in the home but also versatile and applicable to both Japanese and Western cuisines.

topic 7
SHOKUJI DOKORO 和食の食事処
types of washoku restaurants

どこで和食を食べますか？
食堂、料理店、料亭、そして居酒屋

「町じゅうにレストランがある！」と訪日観光客が驚くほど、日本には実にさまざまな食事処があります。和食を食べるなら「食堂」がもっとも気軽です。どんぶり (P.8)、うどん (P.46)、洋食 (P.32)、定食 (P.28) など、幅広いメニューを揃えた"町の食卓"です。寿司 (P.14)、鰻 (P.26)、そば (P.44)、天ぷら (P.24) などは単品に特化した料理店があり、老舗や名店で職人技を堪能できます。フォーマルなディナーや接待の場となるのが、コースを出す会席料理店 (P.38) です。「料亭」は、その最高峰。美しい器 (P.104) への盛り付けだけでなく、花や書画などのしつらい、着物姿での給仕といった、非日常的な演出から、和食の総合芸術を体感できます。

一方、庶民的な夜の食事どころが、居酒屋です。イギリスのパブ、ドイツのビアホール、イタリア、スペインのバルに似ていますが、日本の居酒屋はバーとレストランが合体したような場で、飲むと食べるがオールインクルーシブ。グループ客の利用が多く、活気ある雰囲気は旅行者にも人気です。居酒屋では席につくと「お通し」と呼ばれる小さな料理が運ばれてきます。注文していない料理が出てくることに戸惑う人もいますが、これはお店からのご挨拶のようなものです。居酒屋の定番メニューは、唐揚げ、ポテトサラダ、焼き魚、冷奴、おでん (P.60) など。その日に入荷した旬の食材のお品書きが「本日のおすすめ」として、黒板に掲示されていることがあります。人気の居酒屋ドリンクは、果物のフレーバーをつけた蒸留酒の焼酎のソーダ割り「酎ハイ」。お酒のメニューに地酒があれば、同じ土地で生まれた酒と料理の相性の良さを試してみたいところです。数多いメニューが選びきれなければ、ご主人に予算を伝えて「おまかせ」とお願いするのもいいでしょう。

Ryotei 料亭 *traditional high-class Japanese restaurant*

Tanzakumenyu 短冊メニュー *menu strips*

Where to Eat Japanese Food?
Cafeterias, Restaurants, Ryotei, and Izakaya

"There are restaurants everywhere!" Tourists are often surprised by the various types of restaurants in Japan, among which shokudo, which translates to "canteen," are the most casual. They are the town's eateries with extensive menus, serving classic dishes like donburi rice bowls (*P.8*), udon noodles (*P.46*), and yoshoku (*P.32*) , and teishoku set meals (*P.28*). Specialty restaurants serving specific foods such as eel (*P.26*),

Izakaya Oyaji 居酒屋の親父 *zakaya master*

sushi (*P.14*), soba (*P.44*), or tempura (*P.24*) are often long-established, renowned restaurants where one can experience artisanal cooking. Kaiseki restaurants (*P.38*), of which ryotei are the most sophisticated, serve traditional course meals and are suited for more formal situations or business meals. The vessels (*P.104*), ornamental flowers, paintings and the servers in kimono — everything is orchestrated in an exquisite manner to enable a full experience of the art that Japanese cuisine is.

Izakayas on the other hand are casual dinner spots open late into the evening. Similar to British pubs, German beer halls, or Spanish tapas bars, a Japanese izakaya is both a bar and a restaurant for drinkers and eaters alike. Many customers come in groups, and the lively atmosphere is popular among tourists as well. Upon sitting down at an izakaya, a small appetizer called "*otoshi*" is served. First-timers may be confused by this dish they did not order, but it is considered a greeting from the restaurant. A popular izakaya beverage is *chu-hai*, which is a mixed drink with *shochu* (a distilled alcohol made from potatoes or grains), soda, and fruit flavoring or juice. Classic izakaya menu items include karaage fried chicken, Japanese-style potato salad, grilled fish, cold tofu, and oden (*P.60*). Daily specials featuring fresh seasonal ingredients are often listed on a chalkboard. If local sake or shochu is on the menu, it might be a good idea to sample it along with the local foods and explore how well they match. If the menu is overwhelming, some izakayas will do an *omakase* meal within a customer's budget upon request.

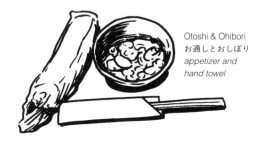

Otoshi & Ohibori
お通しとおしぼり
*appetizer and
hand towel*

WASHOKU

An Illustrated Guide to Japanese Food

世界に教えたい日本のごはん

2021 年 1 月 2 日　初版発行
2024 年 6 月 2 日　2 版発行

編　者	沢田眉香子 Text & Editing: Mikako Sawada	
発行者	伊住公一朗	
発行所	株式会社 淡交社	
	本社　〒603-8588　京都市北区堀川通鞍馬口上ル	
	営業　075（432）5156	
	編集　075（432）5161	
	支社　〒162-0061　東京都新宿区市谷柳町 39-1	
	営業　03（5269）7941	
	編集　03（5269）1691	
	www.tankosha.co.jp	
印刷・製本	シナノ書籍印刷株式会社	

翻　訳	リース恵実 Translation: Emmy Reis	
イラスト	川村淳平 Illustration: Jumpei Kawamura	
デザイン	いわながさとこ Design: Satoko Iwanaga	
カバー写真	伊藤 信 Cover Photography: Makoto Ito